Putting It Together in the Parish

Putting It Together in the Parish

James D. Glasse

Abingdon Press

Nashville   New York

ISBN 0-687-34932-X

Library of Congress Catalog Card Number: 71-185548

Scripture quotations unless otherwise noted are
from the Revised Standard Version of the Bible,
copyrighted 1946 and 1952 by the Division of Christian Education, National Council of Churches,
and are used by permission.

Some of the material in chapters III and XI appeared in the author's article "Seminaries and Professional Education," which was published in
Theological Education, Autumn, 1971.

MANUFACTURED BY THE PARTHENON PRESS AT
NASHVILLE, TENNESSEE, UNITED STATES OF AMERICA

For Joan

Foreword

The Alumni Association and Board of Trustees of Austin Presbyterian Theological Seminary established a lectureship in 1945 to bring to the Seminary campus some distinguished scholar each year to address an annual midwinter convocation of ministers and students on some phase of Christian thought.

The Thomas White Currie Bible Class of Highland Park Presbyterian Church of Dallas, Texas, in 1950, undertook the maintenance of this lectureship in memory of the late Dr. Thomas White Currie, founder of the class and president of the Seminary from 1921 to 1943.

The material given in the Currie Lectures for the year 1970 is included in this volume.

DAVID L. STITT
PRESIDENT
AUSTIN PRESBYTERIAN THEOLOGICAL SEMINARY
AUSTIN, TEXAS

Preface

The present-day pastor has at his disposal a remarkable range of resources. If he can put all this together in the parish he can have a creative and effective ministry. This book is a report of some professional models and strategies that I have observed while watching responsible pastors at work around the country. The emphasis is on getting started, simple disciplines that set the direction for the pastor in his professional development. Many pastors have already moved beyond the starting points I suggest. But many still do not know where or how to start. This book is for them. The disciplines I propose are designed to enable the pastor to "factor out the variables," then "put it all together" in fresh and fruitful ways.

All the material on these pages has appeared somewhere before. The ideas have grown out of, and been tested in, the crucible of encounter with parish ministers across the country. In pastors' schools, seminars for ministers, retreats, workshops, and seminary classes I have used and shamelessly re-used these things. As one might say of a Broadway play—"it has been tried out on the road."

What is written down here was first spoken, then transcribed and edited. I have not tried to conceal the origins —encounters with pastors around the issues of parish ministry. As I write, the same questions are in my mind as when I speak. Is this how it is with you? Will this help in your parish? Can you use this idea? What do you think of trying it this way? How would you explain this? I

9

seek confirmation and correction from the clergy. If, then, keeping the conversational style in print will help, it is all to the good. Where the style is pedantic and stilted, you will know I have not hammered those parts out on the anvil of professional exchange with pastors.

The bulk of the book, though in quite a different form, made up the Currie Lectures at the Austin Presbyterian Theological Seminary in 1970. I am grateful to President David Stitt and his faculty for the invitation to give the lectures and for the added inducement to publish them. The present form of the book emerged in meetings with United Methodist pastors in Michigan and the Dakotas; Brethren pastors in Florida; pastors of the United Church of Christ in Pennsylvania, Maryland, and New York; and an ecumenical group at the Michigan State Pastors Conference. A summary of the material, presented to the first meeting of the Academy of Parish Clergy in April of 1970, appeared in *The Christian Ministry* magazine of January, 1971.

The material on the case method was prepared first of all for a meeting of the Association of Seminary Professors in the Practical Fields (now the Association for Professional Education for Ministry) and has been used extensively with groups of pastors for almost ten years. *The Journal of the Academy of Parish Clergy* printed some of the material in their first volume. The Rev. Arthur Sherman, Director of the Lancaster Seminary Case Method Project, helped revise the material and assisted in the selection of the sample cases.

Mrs. Pat Werhan at Vanderbilt Divinity School, and Mrs. Edna Hafer and Mrs. Nancy Norris at Lancaster Theological Seminary typed the manuscript at the several stages of its development.

My new colleagues in Lancaster—faculty and students in the seminary, pastors in the community—have encouraged me to spell out some of my ideas about ministry and theological education. Although this book is primarily for pastors, I have some ideas about its impact on seminary education, especially at the point of designing new kinds of research in parish dynamics and pastoral practices. Seminaries must become more accountable to the profession. Pastors who use the disciplines outlined here can make a major contribution to the redirection of seminary life toward the church's mission and the ministry's professional development. At Lancaster Seminary we are taking this redirection seriously, specializing in the preparation of pastors for parish churches.

JAMES D. GLASSE
LANCASTER THEOLOGICAL SEMINARY
LANCASTER, PENNSYLVANIA

Contents

I. Toward an Effective Parish Ministry

Many discussions of ministry distinguish between parish ministry as a "traditional" ministry on the one hand, and "experimental" ministries on the other. The parish ministry is also discussed as a "general" ministry, while others are "specialized." This is a distinction I reject as inaccurate and misleading.

I consider the parish ministry to be one of the specialized ministries of the profession. That is what *Profession: Minister* was about—to show how the parish ministry is not the norm for the profession, but one of its specialties. And that is what the Academy of Parish Clergy is about— to provide a way by which pastors, as specialists, can associate for professional development.

Every parish ministry, I believe, is a special ministry, and is potentially experimental. Here is a simple way to state it. Whenever a minister becomes pastor of a congregation, the elements of an experiment are there. Clergymen differ and clergymen change. Congregations differ and congregations change. Communities differ and they change. Therefore it remains to be proved (in the manner of an experiment with variables) what will happen when *this* minister becomes pastor of *this* congregation, in *this* community, at *this* time.

A. AN EXPERIMENTAL PARISH MINISTRY

But the pastor cannot pursue his ministry experimentally unless he can factor out the variables and control

17

them one at a time. Trying to do everything, he proves nothing. Before he can put it all together experimentally he must learn to take it apart. As a simple move in the direction of identifying variables, I refer to three dimensions of ministry: personal, professional, institutional. The distinction is not artificial, but it is more or less arbitrary. The lines are not always clear. But it does allow me to take the thing apart and put it back together again. In this sense, what I am doing in the book is a pattern of what the pastor can do in the parish: take his work apart, look at it, and put it back together in new ways.

When the weight of his work becomes unbearable, he can take out a piece of it and work on it. Putting this piece back in the mix again *changes the mix.* If he can change his work one piece at a time, he may be able to remodel it into manageable form. By the time he has done this, it will be time to pull out another piece and begin the process again.

B. SYMPTOMS AND SYNDROMES

Nobody has to tell parish pastors they have problems. They know this. But they do not always see the outlines of their problems clearly. They are too close to them. I want to suggest some shapes I see in their struggles, some patterns in their perplexities. This requires seeing beneath the symptoms to the underlying syndromes in parish practice.

A symptom is a "sign or token, indicating the existence of something else." We must get to the roots of the "something else." I employ the idea of syndrome, "a group of signs and symptoms that appear together, and characterize a disease." I have discovered two major ones, the *conform/complaint syndrome* and the *bitch/brag syndrome.* Discussions of them appear throughout the book.

A syndrome is not a "problem," but a description of a pattern of behavior which has the character of a disease in that it expresses a kind of uneasiness, a dis-ease. The syndrome develops as a way of coping with a problem, but it tends to lock the pastor into behavior from which he cannot free himself. Describing the dynamics of the syndrome is the first step in putting handles on his problem.

C. THE CONFORM/COMPLAINT SYNDROME

One reaction of pastors to their problems is what I call the *conform/complaint syndrome.* I have discovered this syndrome as a result of my research. (You know that "research" is a term used to legitimate things in the academic community. My research specialty is preacher-watching. I seldom read books about ministers, but I watch a lot of them in action. By observing their actions and listening to their language, I have become an expert preacher-watcher.) I am convinced that the major source of accurate information about the ministry is ministers, themselves. Since I am primarily concerned about the Protestant parish clergy, I spend most of my time watching them. They appear to suffer rather seriously from the symptoms of the conform/complaint syndrome. It appears in many forms. Here is one of them.

A pastor does something he considers irrelevant, useless, stupid, or a waste of time—usually because someone asked him to do it. After he has done it he seeks out a colleague (or his wife) and complains. It goes like this. "Do you know what I did this afternoon? I spent three hours talking to a little old lady. That was a waste of time. Why do I have to do that kind thing? It is such a drag! But that's what people expect of me. If I don't spend a lot of time doing that sort of thing, my people will complain and say

I am not a good pastor. Anyway, she was lonely and I think it helped her to have me just sit there and talk with her for awhile. But I don't have three hours to give to that kind of thing. I have other, more important, things to do."

Note the characteristics of the syndrome: conformity to the expectations of someone else, explanation of why it was necessary, complaint.

A special form of the syndrome is the conform/explain variation. In this form the pastor does not express a complaint, but seeks only to justify and rationalize his behavior. Actually the conform/complaint form is healthier. At least the pastor has decided not to defend his behavior! That is an improvement.

One reason why pastors find it hard to break the syndrome is that they have become such expert explainers and complainers. They learn how to sophisticate and refine the complaint part of the syndrome, but do not learn how to break the conformity part. Seminaries train men in this, raising complaint to a high art. Theological education can serve, not as a means of overcoming passivity and assuming responsibility, but as a device for legitimating continued conformity. The seminary is a place where future leaders are being trained. But the average seminary attracts passive students, subjects them to authoritarian pressures, and turns them out as passive as they came.

D. PRIESTS, PROPHETS, PASTORS

Another thing that locks ministers into this syndrome is a myth about ministerial styles. Many of my students in the seminary think that when they graduate they have only two options in the parish ministry. On the one hand, they can go into a parish, roll over, and play dead. They can be "priests" to their people, loving them, accepting them, agreeing with them, making no waves and causing no trouble. On the other hand, they can enter a parish, shoot off their mouths, and lose their jobs. This, they think, makes them "prophets." As far as I am concerned, these are two alternative ways of copping out, two ways of not making a difference. On the one hand, you bless the status quo (priest). On the other hand, you blast it (prophet). The effect is the same—nothing changes.

A psychologist tells me that we attract a rather high percentage of passive-dependent and passive-aggressive students to seminaries. This is raw material for "priest" types who want to be loved, accepted, supported (passive-dependent) and for "prophet" types who want to be challenged, confronted, and criticized (passive-agressive). If we do not have a better model for ministry than this matched pair of caricatures we can do very little to help seminarians learn how to change themselves, their work, or the church, let alone the community. There must be a model ministers can use. There is. I call it "pastor."

But how can pastors break the pattern of passivity which keeps them from assuming responsibility for themselves? Pastors tell me they feel like they have no real control over who they are and what they do. "They won't let me be myself, I must always act a role." "They won't leave me alone to do my work, I must always run off to do what someone else expects of me." "I can't get anything done, I must run this parish and that takes all my time." In three important dimensions pastors feel trapped and unable to move: personal, professional, institutional. In the sections that follow we will look at some *personal moves* ministers can make to break out of the conform/complaint syndrome, some *professional methods* pastors can develop to assume responsibility for their professional growth and development, and some *parish models* clergy can employ to design parish practice for specialization and experimentation. Along the way I will use some methods that may appear strange or frivolous. So at this point I will say a word about these things before moving on.

E. DEMYTHOLOGIZING PROTESTANT PASTORALIA

One of the problems in getting a clear picture of the practice of parish pastors is the persistence of what I call American Protestant Pastoralia. This is the pastoral folk-wisdom that ministers use to describe their life and work. Collecting pastoralia is one of my hobbies. This is not easy, because pastoralia persists primarily in oral tradition. I therefore have to work like an anthropologist studying primitive societies, with tape recorder and notebook. I am building up quite a collection and may someday gather them into a book, a kind of *Poor Richard's Almanac* for pastors. But for now I will simply sprinkle these pages with samples at appropriate points.

Pastoralia has the character of folk-wisdom. The sayings have the ring of truth about them. They apply to specific instances, but tend to cancel each other out when set side by side. "Look before you leap" is countered by "He who hesitates is lost." "Out of sight, out of mind" is canceled by "Absence makes the heart grow fonder." If we are to use pastoralia for purposes of professional conversation it must be factored out, translated, and otherwise tested to make it into a professional language, a kind of *lingua franca* for pastors.

To assist with the task I have invented an imaginary machine something like a computer. I call it my "demythologizer." It works like this. The machine has several settings, each designed to perform a particular part of the demythologizing function. You push the "reverse" button, and a piece of pastoralia is read back as a pious statement of the opposite. One of my favorite pieces of pastoralia is: "A pastor never knows how much good he is doing." Put this into the demythologizer, push the "reverse" button, and it comes out: "A pastor never knows how much damage he is doing." (Get the idea?)

When pastors do not use this kind of device, the pastoralia simply goes into their own private computers and disappears. It goes like this in a group of pastors. One says: "A pastor never knows how much good he is doing." The others nod knowingly, purse their lips, and say, "Uhmmmmmmmm" or "True, true." There is wisdom in many of the sayings. But they must be demythologized if they are to serve any useful function.

Another setting on the machine is triggered by pushing the button marked "professional." This setting takes a piece of pastoralia and asks: what sense would it make for another professional to make this statement?

A pastor has been in a particular parish for a number of years. One day he is sitting in his study, musing to himself. "I have been pastor of this church for five years. I have had a useful ministry here. But I think I have done about all I can in this place. Perhaps it is time for me to move on."

Put that in the machine, push the "professional" button, and here is what comes out.

Lawyer: "I've been practicing law in this town for five years. I have had a good practice, and done very well. But I think I have done about all I can in this place. Perhaps I should move on." What sense does that make?

Teacher: "I have been teaching third grade for ten years. I have taught a lot of children. But I think I have done about all I can in this school. Perhaps it is time for me to move on." What sense does it make for a teacher to talk like this?

Doctor: "I have been a doctor in this town for seven years. I have helped a lot of people, and improved the services of the hospital. But I think I have done about all I can in this place. Perhaps it is time for me to move on."

You see how it works. It is really very simple. And it can be lots of fun! Most of all it helps identify some of the ways in which the wisdom of the profession is out of phase with the practice of the profession. It raises new questions that must be answered. And it requires us to move beyond demythologizing to the more difficult task of remythologizing. If the old wisdom won't work, what is the new wisdom?

F. THE PROFESSIONAL PERSPECTIVE: PASTORAL EPISTLES

The pastor can free himself from captivity to the conform/complaint syndrome by distinguishing between his personal life and his professional practice. He can separate who he is from what he does. This was stated very nicely by a United Methodist minister in Ohio. After reading *Profession: Minister* he wrote me a letter. Here is part of it.

I have felt that I was neither a very good Christian nor a very good minister. And I think I am seeing for the first time why this is so. It is because I have not been able (or have not thought I ought) to separate my Christian commitment from my professional life. Consequently, my professional work is frustrated by my striving to be a "good Christian" in my work (almost solely through my work, by the way); while my Christian commitment suffers because I have tried to use my professional life as the content of my faith. If the two can be separated, then much of my anxiety would be done away with. You've about convinced me that they can.

I appreciated your attempt to "tell it like it is," rather than to say how it "should be." This is a freeing kind of approach.

I didn't start the church. I didn't ask to come here. All I want to do is deal with what I have, where I am, in the best way I can.

If I can do that I can say sincerely, "Free at last, free at last, thank God Almighty, I'm free at last."

How can the pastor free himself from the temptation to identify his personal faith with his professional practice? Here is a man who knows. He simply adopted a professional attitude, viewed his situation from a professional perspective, and found the answer. If he can do it, so can others.

Another tyranny from which the pastor needs to free himself is a sense of inferiority in relation to his seminary professors, the hierarchy of his denomination, and the "specialized ministries." How this can be done is illustrated by a letter from another pastor. From a small parish in New Hampshire he wrote:

I think there are four primary sources of "professional" guilt as opposed to "personal" guilt. Three originate in seminary training, and the fourth involves denominational relationships.

The first source involves the prevalent seminary attitude toward preaching. A seminarian quickly realizes that speakers at convocations are given honor if they are scholars. But if they are pastors they are considered simply sources of inspiration and emotional manipulation. This produces a conflict in the young minister, since at least 25 per cent of his time is devoted to preaching and he is evaluated primarily on the basis of his preaching ability. One begins to realize that the seminary attitude is unrealistic and that preaching is very important.

The second source of professional guilt is related to the seminary attitude toward the "rites of passage" of the church. One has to overcome the implicit attitude that these things are archaic, and begin to realize that they are symbolic affirmations of the crisis points in the life of the human being. What a difference between this idea and the complaint that people only come to the minister to be baptized, married, and buried.

The third source of guilt comes from the current downgrading of the parish ministry. The value of the parish ministry is seldom a first-hand experience of seminary professors. Undoubtedly the parish ministry needs to be upgraded, but its opportunities are obvious even in this small community. I have come to realize that I have access to families of every social class and (if I wish) can relate professionally to more people in this community than anybody else.

The fourth source of guilt arises out of denominational relationships. The churches of my parish are related to three different denominations. At least 80 per cent of the denominational literature asks me to support some programs beyond my parish. It takes a young man some time to realize that he cannot respond to all these requests. Of course there is a temptation to become as parochial as the parish. Most non-metropolitan parishes like this are considered problems, not promising situations with potential. They are small and do not challenge the full-time capacities of a professional person. This is why self-discipline is critically necessary to maintain professional standards in every aspect of parish ministry.

This is practical theology of a very high order! I have never met these men. I only know that they have begun to find very significant ways to overcome the conform/complaint syndrome. They have developed a respect for themselves and their work. They have begun to free themselves from the tyranny of a false piety, seminary-induced inferiority feelings, and denominational chauvinism. This has not made them arrogant or pretentious. It has freed them for the kind of humble service to which they are dedicated. It is a promising sign that pastors, by adopting a professional perspective, can see through the syndromes.

The way is now open for them to begin breaking out of the syndromes and moving toward a more effective ministry.

Blessed is the pastor who has seen through the syndrome;
he is free to move toward a more effective ministry.

II. Dealing with Change and Calculating Risks

No one needs to be told that we live in changing times. Nor do I need to add to the literature describing the changes that confront us as a culture. I just want to point out how parish pastors can move from a passive to an active stance in relation to change. A *passive stance* in relation to change produces adaptation. An *active stance* produces innovation. The passive pastor will be a *problem-solver,* dealing with those problems and issues that are thrust upon him. He will do what he has to do, when he has to do it, trying always to adapt to the changes so that he is not defeated or destroyed by them. This style might have been effective in a time of slower, simpler change. But it will not do today. The active pastor will become a *problem-seeker,* a pioneer moving toward problems not yet perceived by others nor yet popular in the culture. Either way, he must deal with change.

In order to do this, the pastor must develop professional disciplines that enable him to do at least four things: identify changes in his own parish practice, develop a working theory of change, test his tolerance for change, and become an effective agent of change.

A. IDENTIFYING CHANGES IN PARISH PRACTICE

No one knows who discovered water, but it certainly wasn't a fish! We tend to take for granted things that surround us so completely that they do not stand out. It is hard to see the shape of change these days because it is so pervasive. The first task of the pastor is to develop disciplines of perception by which he can simply see what is going on around him. But how can he do this? He can begin by focusing on changes in his own professional life.

One of the devices I have developed for doing this is a "change-grid." It is designed to help pastors identify specific changes in their own pastoral work, and to see these in relation to the forces and factors that produce change. It asks not for information about the ministry in general, but only about what ministers know firsthand. It asks pastors to think for a few moments about the kinds of changes they have experienced, and to write down their reflections on this simple grid.

Change-grid

1. List some things you are doing *more* of these days, or things you didn't do before:

   Identify the sources of these changes, as best you can under these headings:

   A. *Personal* B. *Ecclesial* C. *Social*

2. List some things you are doing *less* of these days, or things you don't do anymore:

   Identify the sources of these changes:

   A. *Personal* B. *Ecclesial* C. *Social*

It is often helpful to ask the pastors in the group to list a specific number of things, like three items under each heading, or to specify a period of time, like changes in the past five years, or ten years. The purpose of the change-grid is to help the particular pastor identify his own experience of change.

A discussion with a group of pastors using this technique produces three things. *First,* individual pastors begin to see the shape of change in their own ministry. Pastors know that their work-life is changing, but they do not always know how to picture the pattern so it is clear to them. The grid helps. *Second,* the group can see similarities and differences in patterns of change reflected in the several grids. This leads to a discussion of the various types of ministries and a discovery of the way in which different parish settings affect patterns of change in ministry. *Third,* pastors contribute to the descriptive literature about parish ministry which is so badly needed. Beginning with the use of this grid, pastors can begin to reflect more systematically on the nature of the changes in which they are involved. I have discovered that it doesn't do much good to raise general questions like: "How is your ministry changing these days?" General questions get general answers. The first move a pastor must make is to think concretely about his specific situation. On the basis of an increasing number of concrete reports, we can begin to develop a more comprehensive picture of the changes in ministry today. In addition, through the continued use of disciplines like this, we have a method for keeping in touch with the changes. This is, then, another form of parish-based research in which any pastor can participate and to which all pastors can contribute.

B. TOWARD A WORKING THEORY OF CHANGE: FROM STAIRS TO ESCALATORS

Using the change-grid I have discovered that most pastors think of change in terms of a "stair step" theory. History is seen as a series of long periods of stability and order, broken from time to time by revolution. They therefore look for change only in very clear and dramatic forms. They report events that mark very significant shifts, using the language of "before" and "after." "Before I en-

tered the ministry . . . after I graduated from seminary";
"Before the war . . . after the depression."

One of the most important changes to be understood is
the change in the shape of change. First of all, there has
been a change in the *rate* of change. Even if the basic
pattern of change is still in "steps," the time between
changes has become shorter. This makes the rate of change
more rapid. A second change is in the *degree* of change.
Because of developments in communication and trans-
portation, more people can be affected in more ways in
less time. Put in a simple graph, the population explosion
looks like this:

POPULATION EXPLOSION ———— World population is
increasing at an unprecedented rate as the chart shows.

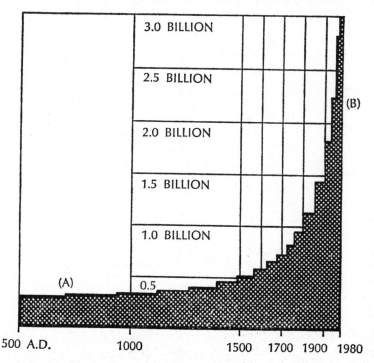

At point A we have a picture of the past, when periods of stability were longer and the amount of change was less. At point B is the shape of change when larger changes take place between shorter periods of stability. Almost everything in modern life can be put on a graph like this: population growth, changes of residence, technical innovation, etc.

This pattern of change is also seen in theological changes in the church. When my father graduated from seminary in 1918 he had a theology that lasted him for forty-five years. I went to seminary after World War II and got one that lasted me about three and a half years. I work on the theory that the half-life of theological systems is now about eighteen months. John Lawing's cartoon in *Christianity Today* put it this way:

Let me introduce Dr. Golfitz, whose ideas controlled European theology briefly in February of 1967.

A pastor put it this way: trying to be a minister these days is a little like a hen trying to lay an egg on an escalator! If the pattern of change is like stair steps, then we have to say that the stairs have started to move. We are on an escalator. This is a pretty good picture. But if this is a good theory of change, it too will change. The pastor must always revise his theory of change to fit the facts of his experience. Therefore he has two continuing tasks: to perceive accurately the changes in which he is involved, and to picture imaginatively the pattern of these changes. But more than perception and understanding are required. The pastor must also act in relation to change.

C. CHANGE AGENT: A NEW ROLE FOR THE PARISH PASTOR

The pastor needs disciplines that test his tolerance for change and train him to be a more effective agent of change. Many pastors discover in using the change-grid that they have adjusted to more changes than they had realized. Identifying degrees of tolerance to change defines adaptive skills. This is a very important kind of change. It is required for the survival of the church as an institution and the ministry as a profession. But the minister must move beyond his passive, adaptive stance. And that means he must be prepared to deal with conflict.

Conflict, I believe, is produced not by the introduction of change, but by resistance to change. This is a debatable thesis. I intend to defend it later, and to describe specific techniques for conflict-management (Chapter IX). At this point I want only to note that conflict is usually a consequence of change. The pastor will want to be prepared to deal with it constructively and imaginatively when it comes. Training in "conflict management" is available in many places these days. An inquiry to judicatory staff, national agency, or nearby seminary is the way to begin.

D. CALCULATING RISKS

If a minister is going to change, he will run some risks. Some would argue that the minister runs risks if he *doesn't* change. Either way, risk-taking is a thing the minister must learn to do. Of course, the minister is always running risks. But he is not always aware of what he is doing. Becoming self-conscious about risk-taking is the first step.

One of the barriers to seeing the problems and possibilities is the fog of folk-wisdom that engulfs the profession. Pieces of pastoralia get in the way. Here is one of them:

> *"I can't say/do that. If I did I would run the risk of losing members/money/my job, or creating conflict."*

Thus do many pastors protect themselves against having to think about the concrete consequences of their actions. The possibility of risk is invoked as a reason not to think or act. It is a very effective device. But take that piece of pastoralia, put it into the demythologizer, push the "reverse" button. It comes out like this:

> *"If I* don't *say/do that, I would risk losing members/ money/my job, and creating conflict."*

Demythologizing that piece of pastoralia doesn't help much. It leaves us right where we were, with nowhere to go. So we try another setting on the machine to "factor out the variables." It comes out like this.

*If I say/do what?*_____
I will run a _____% *risk*
of losing _____ *members (name them)*
*and $*_____ *money*
and a _____% *risk of losing my job.*

That's a beginning. It breaks the situation down to the point where simple, factual questions can be asked and concrete, calculable answers can be given. This is a move into the situation that can enable the pastor to pursue the problem professionally.

The pastor must be able to *calculate the risk* if he is to run the risk responsibly. This requires the construction of an "equation" by which the risk can be calculated. With practice any pastor can learn to do it. Here is a way to start.

E. AN EQUATION FOR CALCULATING RISKS

Within a month after entering a new parish (and at least annually) the pastor should make a rough calculation of the risks he will have to run to achieve the objectives he has set for himself. As a first step he must calculate what he is prepared to lose in any risk. A simple formula for the calculation might include the following.

1. How many members he can afford to lose, and still maintain a viable congregation. He should also identify particular members he can most afford to lose and those he can least afford to lose.

2. How much money he can afford to lose from the church budget, and the effect of the loss of particular members on the predicted income of the congregation.

3. How much personal income he can afford to lose and still meet his financial obligations. What additional sources of income are available to him if he should lose

more than the estimated amount, and the things he is prepared to give up if the money runs out.

4. How much public acceptance, respect, and affection he is prepared to sacrifice for his convictions. Which sectors of the public are most important to him: parishioners, fellow pastors, community leaders.

5. How much public censure he and his family can tolerate, including the number of obscene phone calls per week his wife can stand, and the amount of ostracism his children can endure.

6. How much physical danger he is prepared to suffer, if need be, including the risk to his life and that of his family.

This may sound melodramatic and overdrawn. It is meant to press the outer limits of risk. But I know ministers who have learned to think this way. Not only in the South, under pressure of severe racial tensions, but increasingly in communities across the country, pastors are beginning to count the cost of their convictions and to calculate their risks.

If the pundits are right, there will be a decline in the religious establishment. In simple economic terms this may mean that ministers will not be paid so well in the future—that it will "cost" them to be pastors, not just "pay" them.

The pastor who says, "I will do nothing that might lose the love and respect of my people," has said a mouthful. He has given "his people" absolute veto power over all his activities. He has set an equation with a constant of "zero" in it. He has stated the terms of his personal equation for calculating risks. Zero times anything is always zero!

The pastor who says, "I will do what is right, no matter what it costs me," has also said a mouthful. He has given himself an ultimatum that he may live to regret. He may have committed his wife and family to a course of action in which they cannot concur, and from which he might not survive.

In these two extreme examples we have another instance of the stylized ministerial models referred to earlier. The first is a caricature of the "priest," who thinks all he can do is roll over and play dead. The second is a caricature of the "prophet," who thinks all he can do is shoot off his mouth and lose his job. What both have in common is a commitment to the status quo. The effect of each is the same: to leave things just as they are, unchanged.

F. ON LIVING TO FIGHT ANOTHER DAY

When a "prophetic" type blows his job, "priestly" types will purse their lips, nod their heads, and say sagely: "You have to be around here awhile before you can do certain things."

Now there's a piece of "pastoralia" that cries out for demythologizing. It is so obviously true that it must be understood. But it is so completely abstract that we must factor out the folklore before it can be used. So I put it in my demythologizer, push the button for "factoring" folklore, and wait for the results. Out comes the tape. It reads:

> *How long . . . must who . . . be around where . . . doing what . . . before who . . . can do what . . . to whom . . . with what specific consequences . . . and how do you know when you have been there that long?*

If we can factor out the folklore, we can ask some sensible questions. The critical questions, in light of this discussion of risks, have to do with how much risk the pastor is prepared to run. If to "do certain things" means to "get away" with something there is little willingness to pay the price. If the "certain things" are words to be spoken, then the pastor needs to ask how much he still believes in word magic, or how much he is confusing the model of "professor" with that of "prophet."

Any pastor who wants to effect significant social change must calculate how much time it will take to do what he wants to get done. This will often mean slowing down his personal timetable, but just as often it may mean speeding it up. Using this piece of pastoralia with the folklore factored out can help start the process.

G. EXPERIMENTS IN CHANGE

Learning to calculate risks is one way of learning how to change things. A pastor who wants to effect change must have at least the ability to stay in one place long enough to make a difference. He must also have some perception of his own objectives. In addition, he must have basic skills in calculating the possible effect of his actions. This is what lies behind the need to learn how to calculate risks. If he can learn this, he can begin to experiment with strategies for change. If he knows that he must walk that fine line between losing his vision and losing his job, he has learned the first lesson. Then he can begin to experiment.

He does not have to deal with global goals. He does not fear "losing members," because he has calculated how many he can afford to lose. He does not fear "losing money," because he knows how much he can afford to risk. He has set the limits of the risks he is prepared to run, and he can now calculate the possible effects of his actions within responsible limits. If he fears the loss of twenty members because of a particular action, and discovers that he has lost only ten—he has miscalculated in his own favor. Of course, it could go the other way! But either way it goes he has a way to work at his ministry that frees him to design experiments—even risky and dangerous ones—which test the limits of his professional competence and free him to move beyond a meager professionalism to a mature professionalism.

Some ministers want to be "prophetic" without being "professional." I do not know how a man can do this responsibly. When you are asking people to change, you are asking them to run risks. You cannot ask others to do what you are not willing to do yourself. Your risks are different from those of laymen. Your professional life is at stake. This shapes your involvement and your commitment. It limits you at some points, frees you at others. The pastor who wants to move into a professional style can begin by learning how to calculate and run risks.

Instead of being a passive problem-solver, responding only to the options shaped by others and pressed on him by others, the pastor can be a problem-seeker, designing his own experiments for professional action. He can set his own objectives and evaluate his own performance.

Blessed is the pastor who sets his own objectives; he knows what he is doing.

III. Developing a Professional Career

Another way to break out of the conform/complaint syndrome, to overcome the passivity that plagues the parish clergyman, is to focus on the development of the professional *career*.

Most pastors feel trapped at some point in their career. So it may help pastors to know that there is a career pattern in the ministry, that the crisis points are known, and that help is on the way. There are three crisis points in most clergymen's careers.

A. THREE PREDICTABLE CRISES

1. The first three to five years in the ministry is a period of initiation into the profession. It is a time of testing and experimentation. The young pastor has spent almost all his life in schools. He has learned a lot about this situation and has developed the skills required in it. (See the discussion of skill and situational specialization in *Profession: Minister* pp. 117-18.) He is an expert in reading books, writing papers, and passing examinations. In the parish he is seldom asked to do these things!

The young minister must now learn an entirely new role. He is no longer student-in-school but pastor-in-parish. He is seldom trained for this transition, and it is quite a shock. It is only natural that he will wonder whether he has entered the right profession. So, after three to five years he begins to wonder: Should I stay in this kind of work or get out?

At this point the pastor has a decision to make. If he does not make it cleanly, the unresolved questions will continue to haunt him. One temporizing move many ministers make is to try another kind of ministry. After three years in a rural parish, the thought of life in the city is attractive. So the young minister may accept a position as staff member in a larger church. Or, after three years as assistant to a senior minister, the young man may feel the itch to "have his own church." This will enable him to move to another setting, to adopt another role, and to confront again the question of his "place" in the ministry.

By this time his family responsibilities have increased. He has begun to lose some of his freedom to move. The options open to him are a little clearer. He resolves the crisis by leaving the ministry, changing his ministerial specialty, or confirming his original commitment—and moves toward the second crisis.

2. At about age forty the pastor reaches "the point of no return." By now it is clear not only *that* he has a place in the ministry, but *what* that place is. He also knows that he has gone about as far as he will go. And he knows that if he remains in the ministry, it will be twenty more years of pretty much the same thing. He has to ask himself: is this what I want to do for twenty years? Many will answer "yes" and move on to fruitful ministries. Others will say "no"—and leave the ministry. Some do not decide but simply stay and act out the conform/complaint syndrome.

3. Then at sixty or sixty-five comes the time to retire. Most ministers are not ready for it, either financially or emotionally. But there are signs of healthy new develop-

ments. Church pension plans, along with social security, provide the possibility of a comfortable retirement. Parttime jobs encourage men to leave the ministry at sixty, rather than sixty-five, thus opening up parishes for younger men.

But it is no easier to get out of an occupation than it is to get in. Three to five years before retirement the pastor faces the same problems he faced in the first three to five years of his ministry—only in reverse. At the beginning of his career he was trying to work his way into the profession. Now he must work himself out. This is where a professional attitude during one's career is an aid to handling this crisis. If one's commitment to ministry is too personal, it frustrates competence along the way and complicates retirement at the end.

Knowing these simple facts about the clergy career can help a pastor plan his life realistically. He can brace himself for the crises, and deal with them when they come. He can resolve the issues appropriate to each crisis and not have to wrestle with the whole package at the same time. And, by sharing this common knowledge with colleagues, he can find support from fellow pastors in the process.

A new resource for pastors is a network of "career centers" developing across the country. The Northeast Career Center in Princeton, New Jersey, was the pioneer effort. Under the direction of the Reverend Thomas E. Brown, this center has set the pace and charted the course for a whole new movement. A Career Development Council has been organized to coordinate the work of these centers. For information about these centers and their services, pastors may write to the Lancaster Career Development Center, P.O. Box 1529, Lancaster, Pennsylvania 17604.

B. CONTINUING EDUCATION AND CAREER DEVELOPMENT

Another way a pastor breaks out of the conform/ complaint syndrome is to seek further education and training. But even in doing this he may not find the freedom he seeks. Many programs in continuing education for pastors are regressive, calling for the minister to return to school, live in the dormitory, sit at the feet of the professor, study in the library, and return again to his parish with a term paper and a set of notes.

Pastors must assume responsibility for their own professional self-development, and one move they can make is to get together in groups. The technical term for this is "collegiality." It is now being used by the Academy of Parish Clergy to identify one of the moves ministers can make. But I learned something important about it from the building engineer at our school! I noticed one day that he looked very tired, and asked him what was the matter. He told me that he was going to school three nights a week and it was wearing him out. Of course, I asked him what he was doing. He told me that he and ten other men, building superintendents from all over the city, had gotten together, paid $200 apiece, and employed an instructor to train them in new methods of air-conditioning operations. When they completed the course, they would be certified to supervise larger and more complex machines and be qualified for new jobs or for upgrading in their present posts. I asked myself: when was the last time a dozen pastors got together and paid out even $10 apiece to hire someone to teach them something they wanted to know?

Pastors can continue to take advantage of continuing education programs offered by seminaries, state universities, denominational agencies, judicatories, etc. But pastors must assume responsibility for deciding what they need, then go out and find it. The Academy of Parish Clergy can assist pastors, but pastors can also do it for themselves. In a sense, continuing education cannot contribute to career development until the pastor assumes responsibility.

Change-grid: *Planning Professional Development*

Here is a simple device I use to get pastors into this task. I ask them to reflect on a series of simple questions, set down their thoughts, and share them with a group. This is another form of the change-grid.

1. What will your job be like in five years? personal/ ecclesial/social.
2. What specific skills will you need?
3. How can these be learned? Can you learn on the job, or must you get special training?
4. Where will you find the time, money, to get the necessary training?

Once again, simple questions require the pastor to identify his own objectives. In this way he can break out of the conform/complaint syndrome to a kind of professional autonomy that frees him to move out of a passive professionalism. Otherwise he can continue to read the irrelevant books, attend the senseless seminars, or sit in his study—and complain.

C. NON-CAREERS IN THE MINISTRY

This kind of talk about career development will not make much sense to pastors attracted to the ministry by certain images. These images tend to attract non-learners to a life of non-learning, and non-changers to a life of non-change.

Take the "fearless prophet" of the evangelical tradition: the man with unchangeable convictions who does not follow the crowd, who "takes his stand" and, come what may, stands there. He never listens, he never learns, he never moves; and we want him to be a change agent! All he can change is his stuffed shirt.

Then there's the "pious pipeline": the big believer, the one who *really* believes. He knows that what sets ministers off from laymen is that ministers believe a lot and laymen just believe a little. Ministers are professional believers! I submit that it is theologically unsound to assume that a clergyman in the Protestant tradition has to be anything more than an ordinary Christian when it comes to be-lieving. He really doesn't have to have any more "religion" than anybody else, but he has to have more "theology." Our symbol system is demonic if it tends to encourage anyone to think that he'll become more religious by be-coming a clergyman. Some students think they will *get religious* by going to seminary. Maybe some of them do— but a lot of them don't. Some ministers seem to think that they *stay religious* by being ministers. You know, there may be some truth in that! I used to think that the min-istry was God's gift to those among us who were the most faithful and the most dedicated. I've come to believe that maybe just the opposite is true: that the ministry is God's occupational concession to some of the weak and wavering among us who half suspect that if it wasn't our job to do so, we wouldn't read the Bible, we wouldn't be nice to people, and we wouldn't even go to church.

Another ministerial model is what I call the "ecclesiasti-cal hippie": the man who goes around doing his "thing." The ecclesiastical hippie does his thing, and when his thing doesn't work any more, he goes somewhere else and does his thing, and when *they* get bored he goes some-where else and does his thing. One of the symptoms is a way of talking about his career development. He may say: "I've been here three or four years and I think my work here is done. It's time for me to move on to some other [meaning larger] field of service." This man, fifteen years in the business, has moved three times. He hasn't had fifteen years experience; he's had five years experience three different times! He never has to change anything but his location. He never learns, he never grows; he doesn't have to. The system is designed to maximize his idiosyncrasies and make it possible for him to keep alive the illusion of his creativity simply by moving around. This is a poor model for continuing education. It encourages geographical movement, not professional growth.

Then there's the "pastor who knows and loves his people." Bless his heart! This fellow runs around the parish getting to know everybody's name, whose cousin is married to whom, and all that. Then he leaves with no records for his successor so that the other fellow will have to go through the same moves to collect the same information. He never really gets to know anybody, and seldom does anything for them except remember their birthdays. He can usually convince himself that he is "knowing and loving people," but he never really learns anything. And he contributes nothing to the learning of his colleagues.

The question of "collegiality" is not the issue here, but dealing with patterns of ministerial succession is one way into that question. What information should a pastor leave for his successor? Can pastors, as professionals, share professional information within the framework of "professional confidences"? We must move in that direction. In the meantime I hope pastors can find ways to leave relevant information about parishes and parishioners for their successors. I moved to a parish and found a beautiful map in the pastor's study. On it my predecessor had carefully located all the members of the congregation with pins of different colors—but he didn't leave a "key" to the map. I had no way to know what the yellow, red, white, green, and blue pins meant. I had to pull out all the pins and start over. Right then and there I decided I would never do that to a successor.

We have, you see, plenty of images and models and concepts which are designed precisely to keep people from learning while legitimating their rigidity, their insensitivity, their stupidity, and their piosity. What we need are moves ministers can make which get them in touch with themselves as persons, their work as professionals, and the parish as an institution. Developing a career strategy is one of them.

D. CAREER DEVELOPMENT AND THEOLOGICAL EDUCATION

The seminary is not only a significant "point of entry" into the profession but also provides a significant "rite of passage" as part of the total professional career. Under normal circumstances the candidate for the ministry attends the seminary during his early twenties. This puts him somewhere between late adolescence and early young adulthood. This is a very trying time for most persons in our culture—especially white, Protestant males, who make up the bulk of our seminary population. And the seminary normally extends only three years. This means that theological education in the seminary can be seen as one part of a total career pattern. It is a very small part in terms of time, but it may be a very large part in terms of influence. Put, perhaps too simply, the function of the seminary is to turn them up (recruit), sort them out (admissions), shape them up (teaching), shake them down (examinations), and pass them on (graduation and placement). We are dealing, therefore, with a fairly complex part of a rather long process. Career development provides a model for perceiving and analyzing some of the important parts of the process.

My primary concern as a theological educator is to refute the contention that the function of professional education is to prepare a person for a lifetime of practice, and to support the contention that the purpose of such education is to provide the education necessary for entry into the profession with the basic competence necessary to assume responsibility for professional self-development.

In relation to theological education for ministry it is quite simple: to prepare the seminarian for ordination and entry into his first position with the competence necessary to function effectively in that position for from three to five years, at which time he will make his first major career decision. Beyond that point he is on his own in a world we cannot predict, in a profession that will change significantly, and as a person who will grow and change. This may not sound so challenging as the old call to prepare for a lifetime, but it is much more demanding. It requires an educational system much more comprehensive and pluralistic, more flexible and adaptable. But it allows both professor and student to focus their efforts much more precisely. Because there are really only a very few "points of entry" into the profession. Despite all the talk about the many varieties of ministry today, the range of options for the graduating seminarian are rather limited. Other options will open up along the way—but the seminary cannot train for those because they do not exist for the student.

I really want to bear down on this: many of us have been terribly irresponsible in holding out options for students which just don't exist. Admissions officers have often painted pictures of possibilities which were more fiction than fact. And some seminary faculties have been irresponsible in suggesting that almost anybody should study in the seminary if he is interested in religion. Some seminarians drift around the school for three years thinking they are never going to have to work in a church. Then they discover that about 90 percent of the paying jobs open to seminary graduates are in local churches. With a wife and child to support, they rush around during their last year trying to get ready for a job they never thought they wanted and for which they have not prepared. 'It is a miracle we have as few dropouts as we do considering the poor career advice many seminarians receive. We must de-escalate the fantasy level at which many seminary professors and students think about professional options. I am persuaded there are really only four major options. Each provides a focus for the professional education of students. They suggest not "curriculum," but rather "career paths" that students can select and along which faculty can assist the students toward professional self-development. These are the main things a seminary graduate can do with a theological degree:

1. He can become pastor of a church. We know pretty well the kind of church that will call or accept the appointment of a seminary graduate. It will be relatively small, so he need not know how to handle the organizational problems of a congregation of more than 300 members, and he will seldom have a budget in more than five figures. It will be in one of three sociological settings: either out in the boondocks where the population is static or declining; in the inner city where the congregation is static or declining; or in a suburb where the struggling new church is so poor that it can only afford a young seminary graduate. We can prepare a student to minister in this kind of situation with the minimal professional competence required to get him on his way.

2. He can join the staff of a church: either as one of

several staff members on a "last-hired, first-fired" basis; or
the single assistant minister to a relatively competent and
anxious middle-aged pastor who wants someone he can
put down or run to death. We can prepare a student for
this kind of function, with a pretty clear idea of where he
can go from there at the time of his first career decision.

3. He can go into a "specialized" or "experimental"
ministry. If there ever were many jobs like this for seminary graduates (and there were not), there will be fewer
in the future as support funds are in short supply and it
becomes apparent that the ordinary theological education
does not usually equip for these ministries. But if they
exist, the seminary could prepare a man for them.

4. He can go to graduate school. Whether extending his
adolescence, continuing the moratorium on vocational
decision, or preparing for transition to a teaching ministry,
his point of entry is graduate school. For this purpose he
needs no professional training for ministry. But if the job
market pattern in higher education continues, he would
be wise to get some preparation for one of the other points
of entry. Even with a Ph.D. he may end up in a parish—
ready or not.

Since admission to the seminary is a part of admission to
the profession, the seminary must find ways to keep its
programs of recruitment, training, and placement in phase
with the realities of the profession. This will require close
attention to the career patterns of ministers, careful research into the competence required for effective professional functioning, and serious experimentation in
methods of teaching that evoke and nurture these competences. The most the seminary can do is prepare its
graduates for the first three to five years of their careers,
with the disciplines required for professional self-development beyond that point.

Attention to career patterns will also guide the seminary in the development of programs of continuing education. We have learned from recent research about the predictable crises in the career of most clergy. At these points the seminary can contribute to the professional self-development of ministers if they understand the nature of the career crises and respond to them. Simply encouraging ministers to return to the seminary for "further study" or for "getting up to date" will not do. The seminary must find ways to relate to ministers as professional colleagues, not as former students who must remain passive to the professors. This will require some changes in the seminary, itself. Not only the students, but the seminary, must become accountable to the profession. This will require attention to the development of a clearer self-image by the student as he wrestles with his Christian vocation and his occupational identity.

At Lancaster Seminary we have set up the Lancaster Career Development Center. Under the direction of Thomas Brown and the staff of the Center, we are designing a program to introduce seminarians to career development as part of their career in the seminary. The Center will assume responsibility for the testing program and will assist the faculty in developing skill in career counseling as part of the faculty advisory system. They will also guide the development of continuing education for ministers, helping us learn to use career development as a model for theological education.

The responsibility of the seminary, it seems to me, is to assist the student in the assumption of responsibility for his own career development, providing those resources that will help him learn how to learn when he is not in school, and pointing to those career crises we can predict with a plan for dealing with them. With this kind of orientation, students graduating from the seminary will more likely become self-directing professionals, prepared to develop their own careers.

Blessed is the pastor who plans his career: he knows where he is going.

IV. Living in the Maintenance/ Mission Bind

The conform/complaint syndrome has three main forms. Personal: the complaint that conformity to the ministerial role limits the pastor's freedom to "be himself." Professional: the complaint that conforming to the expectations of parishioners keeps the pastor from doing his "proper work." Institutional: the complaint that so much effort goes into "keeping the show on the road" that there is little left over for mission and ministry outside the parish program. I call this form of the syndrome the maintenance/ mission bind.

The pastor wouldn't have any problems if he could find a parish where the people would let him be himself, do what he wanted to do, and keep the show on the road without any help from him. But parishes like that are hard to find. The pastor who spends much time looking for one is wasting his time.

Later on I will suggest some professional methods and some parish models that help the pastor break out of the conform/complaint syndrome. At this point I want to describe one more personal move ministers can make to find the freedom for an experimental ministry in the parish. I call it "paying the rent."

A. PAYING THE RENT

There is a popular story about the husband who, suspecting his wife of an affair, came home early one day hoping to catch her with her lover. She appeared to be alone—and said she was—but the suspicious husband decided to search the house. Finding a strange man in the bedroom closet, he demanded: "What are you doing here?" The man replied: "Everybody's got to be someplace!"

And indeed they do. Since I am concerned primarily to deal with the problems of parish clergy I will not dwell at length with ways other kinds of ministers get to "be someplace." But a brief mention of some of them will provide a frame of reference for what follows.

In business a man can inherit, buy, build, or rent. He can also become an organization man and operate a local branch for a national company. Each of these suggests approaches for the clergyman. Inheriting a place is rare, but not impossible. Adam Clayton Powell inherited the Abyssinian Baptist Church from his father. But he had to maintain it as his own. Church buildings are sometimes for sale, but congregations are not. If a minister wants to go it alone he can become an "ecclesiastical entrepreneur" after the fashion of Oral Roberts, Billy Graham, and others who have set out on their own to "build their own place." But for most ministers a parish is the main option. Every pastor must pay rent in some parish to earn his right to be creative, prophetic, or whatever else he wants to be.

Some professional possibilities exist outside the parish structures of the church. Military, prison, and hospital chaplains are supported by the institutions in the public sector that employ them. Campus ministers, church council executives, and denominational bureaucrats are supported by the organizations they serve. College and seminary teachers earn their pay in the groves of Academe. Although these ministries are not supported directly by parishes, each is set in some institutional context, and the minister must pay the rent required by that institution for his opportunity to serve.

There are some openings for ministers in "experimental ministries," but not many. And the few that still operate are in trouble for lack of funds. Unless they can learn to maintain themselves they will be in deeper trouble.

It is not that the parish pastor is accountable to an institution and other ministers are not. The pastor is accountable to a particular institution, the parish. Everybody's got to be someplace. And everybody has some "rent" to pay. The question is: How to calculate the rent that is to be paid (maintenance) and how does paying this rent free the pastor for service (mission). Therefore the pastor needs some kind of equation for calculating the rent due in the parish in which he serves.

B. CALCULATING THE RENT

The "rent" for a parish consists of more than the congregation demands of its pastor. The pastor has a responsibility to maintain his whole ministry. That includes himself (physical, mental, spiritual) and his professional practice (skill and situational specialties), as well as parish maintenance (which includes the involvement of the parish in the larger mission of the church).

So the simplest form of the equation has three factors: personal, professional, institutional. Each pastor must supply the terms of the equation, taking into account the particular requirements of himself and his family, the special demands at a given point in his professional career, and the unique requirements of the local parish.

It appears to me that most parishes want three things of their pastor. If he meets these minimal requirements he is free to do almost anything else he wants to do. Once he has "paid the rent" he can march for peace, fly an airplane, devote himself to youth problems in the community, paint pictures, pursue advanced education, play a lot of golf, work for the denomination—almost anything. But first he must provide three things:

1. Preaching and worship. People over forty-five are especially serious about this. What they want is a Sunday service that is acceptable, and to which they are not ashamed to invite their friends. They don't expect "great preaching," but they do demand professional performance.

2. Teaching and pastoral care. This does not mean providing cut-rate psychotherapy or frenetic pastoral visitation. But parishioners want to know that the pastor cares for them and is available to them when they have need of him. In teaching, the concern is mainly for the young, but many folk want a man who can stimulate their intellectual understanding of the faith, too.

3. Organization and administration. What most parishes want, and have a right to expect, is a stable membership, a balanced budget, a building in reasonable repair, and organizational leadership that assists them in their parish mission.

I am convinced that a pastor who delivers these basic services has "paid the rent" in the parish. What he and the parish must understand is that "paying the rent" is not a full-time job.

C. MINISTRY IS MORE THAN MAINTENANCE

While there are some situations (what I call the "high rent district") in which the survival of the parish is the complete commitment of the congregation, it needs to be shown whether this is an adequate mission strategy for any parish. If there is nothing left after paying the rent, then the parish must consider whether it has any reason to exist. The purpose of maintenance is to prepare the parish for mission and ministry, just as the purpose of paying the rent is to free the pastor for an extended ministry.

The pastor may feel that, in order to justify a full-time salary, he must devote all his time to his parishioners. But this is a faulty notion. The model of the "ten-tither congregation" illustrates the fallacy.

I think it was Will Campbell who first introduced me to the idea that any ten families who get together and tithe can support a full-time professional ministry. Notice, I did not say "full-time church," but "full-time ministry." It could work like this. Ten families decide they want to be a congregation and support a full-time professional ministry. In trying to figure out how they can do this, a very simple idea emerges. If each family were to tithe (contribute 10 percent of its income) they could employ a pastor at a salary equal to their average income. To make the calculation simple, assume that each family makes $10,000 a year. Each family puts up $1,000, and they have $10,000 to pay a minister. He plays the game by the same rules, so he contributes $1,000 to the parish. They have, therefore, a full-time pastor, $1,000 for operating expenses, and they can meet in anyone's house or garage. (In this sense this model corresponds to a "house church.") This parish does not need a building. If they want to "go to church," the town is already full of churches with empty pews, happy to welcome visitors. Their children can attend the Sunday school and youth fellowships of churches anywhere in the area. Adults can find plenty of choirs to sing in, couples groups to go to, organizations to join. The town probably doesn't need any more of that kind of thing anyway. And anyone interested in a mission-oriented parish probably doesn't want much of it to begin with.

It is interesting to test this idea with pastors. One common reaction is: "That's a great idea! I'd like that $10,000 a year. But what would I do with my time?" The secret is out. The pastor assumes that he works full-time for the people who pay his salary! But the congregation may decide to offer the ministry of their pastor to the community. He can counsel drug addicts, organize the poor, serve as chaplain at a prison. He can do anything that needs doing. He will probably pay some "parish rent" by rendering some pastoral services to the congregation. But most of all he will seek to assist the parish to discover and fulfill a significant ministry in the community.

This model makes it clear that many of the trappings traditionally associated with the parish are not required. As the rate of social change increases and new forms of ministry emerge, it should be encouraging to us all to know that in addition to the promise that wherever two or three are gathered together Christ will be in the midst, there is the prospect that wherever ten or a dozen families get together and tithe, there can be a congregation that decides they want a pastor who will pay the rent to the world and not just to them!

This is not such a radical idea. Even in the quaint terminology we Presbyterians use to call our pastors, the congregation covenants to pay the pastor "that competent worldly maintenance" so he will be "free from all worldly care" to "devote (himself) wholly to the ministry of the gospel." There is a difference between devoting oneself *wholly* to the ministry of the gospel and devoting oneself *solely* to the service of a single parish!

D. KEEPING THE BOOKS ON THE BALANCE

The pastor must pay the rent required by the parish that supports his ministry. This is the first responsibility of the pastor. If he doesn't do it he should be fired or have his salary cut. But after he has paid the rent, what will he do?

At Lancaster Seminary we are trying to learn how to train pastors so they can pay the rent in an average parish in from thirty to forty-five hours per week. That means devoting ten to fifteen hours per week to paying each part of the "bill" submitted by the parish. That is only two to three hours per day, five days per week for each function. Is this possible? We think so. But it will require most pastors to become much more disciplined and efficient than they have ever dreamed! If he is to have any time left over after paying the rent he must become much more efficient in these operations. The trick is not to find more time. There just isn't any more. The task is to learn to discipline your day so you do first things first, and do them quickly and well. You pay the rent to yourself in devotions and study. You pay the rent to the profession by turning your pastoral duties into professional self-development. You pay the rent to the parish by performing necessary services. And you take time for leisure and recreation, for your wife and family, and for community service.

One point of contention between pastor and people in calculating the rent concerns the community activities of the pastor. This issue comes up in two forms. First, in the question about the *kind* of community activity in which the pastor should get involved. A layman who would approve his spending a lot of time with the Boy Scout Council might disapprove his spending any time at all with the Welfare Rights Organization. Second, a question can be raised about the *amount* of community activity in which the pastor should become involved. At this point a simple rule of thumb might be helpful. And it is one every layman will understand. In most congregations there is a general idea about how much time a "dedicated layman" will spend in the work of this church. This activity in the church is his commitment of voluntary service outside his job and family commitments. Most laymen have a pretty clear idea about this, because they calculate it in their own lives. So let the pastor establish the principle that he should, as a responsible citizen, spend as much time in community activities as the layman is expected to spend in church activities. This will not solve the problem, of course. But it can provide a point of reference by which pastor and people can calculate the rent the pastor is expected to pay to the parish while recognizing his need to have some voluntary commitments in the community outside his job and family commitments.

Too many pastors think they have no right to labor as "ordinary men." Others really try to play God—assuming that they can find twenty-five hours a day, thirty-five days a month, and a hundred years to do their work. This is not only bad religion, it is poor professionalism. Until a man can master his calendar and his schedule, and discipline his work to meet his minimal obligations within manageable limits, he will not be able to find that margin for ministry which allows him to move toward a more creative and effective ministry.

E. WHAT TO DO WHEN THE RENT IS PAID

The pastor can use the margins of time and energy he has earned in two ways. He can re-invest his earnings in the same activities on which he has paid the rent. He can devote more time to preaching and worship, to teaching and pastoral care, to administration and organization. But he can do this only after paying all the rent. He cannot borrow from preaching to pay pastoral care, except in emergencies. But if he is a disciplined professional he can "balance his books" at least once a month, redress imbalances, and experiment with other ways to get his basic work done. Re-investing is all right. Every pastor could profit from more attention to his basic parish functions. But there is more to ministry than maintaining the parish.

The second way he can use the freedom he has earned is to expand the range of his ministry, move into mission. He can undertake responsibilities outside his parish. He doesn't have to worry about thinking up things to do. There are already more demands on his time than he can meet. After he has paid the rent and re-invested in parish functions all he wants to, there is still a lot to do.

Blessed is that pastor who has paid his rent;
he has time to give to other pursuits!

V. Driving the Demons from the Datebook

Many ministers complain that they do not have enough time to do their work. It is not that they do not work hard. Most studies of the way ministers use their time show that pastors work long hours. What are pastors to do?

There are two problems, it seems to me: first, facing the fact that there is not enough time; second, finding better ways to use the time that is available. The first one is the hardest to handle for most pastors, because it has deep roots in the folklore of the profession and in the "Protestant work ethic."

There is a lot of arrogance that masquerades as humility in the ministry. The pastor who runs frantically from task to task often acts as if he thinks he could, if he just had the time, do everything for everybody. Although he may see himself as a humble man, simply a servant of others, he is actually acting out a pernicious form of pride.

I know pastors who actually schedule themselves to be in two places at the same time! The pastor could keep that kind of commitment if he had the gift of omnipresence. But, according to my understanding of the Christian religion, that is an attribute reserved for deity. The pastor who programs himself for omnipresence is simply presumptuous. The Bible calls that "sin." The pastor, therefore, ought not try to organize that behavior, but repent of it. The pastor must first of all stop trying to play God.

It sounds simple, but it is not easy to break habits of long-standing.

I am tempted to preach a sermon at this point, calling pastors to repent of their attempts to play God. It should be enough to point out that God himself, according to the Scriptures, created the heavens and the earth in six days— and took a day off. Some pastors act as if they feared the creation would come to a halt if they took a day off. But I know it would not help to preach such a sermon to pastors. What is needed are practical steps the pastor can take to tame his time and drive the demons from his datebook.

A. EXEGETING THE ENGAGEMENT BOOK

One point at which the conform/complaint syndrome appears is in the datebook of the pastor. "Why do I have to go to all these meetings?" he will complain, "I never have any time for myself or my family!" If the question is real, and not just rhetorical, he should be able to answer it. But so long as his complaining gets him sympathy, he will keep on conforming. So he must ask himself some simple and direct questions.

First, raise questions about *specific items*. Why am *I* going to *this* meeting *tonight?* Could I have prepared someone else to lead the meeting? Am I really needed? What would happen if I got sick and couldn't go? Who would know the difference? What difference would it make? Asking this kind of commonsense question about a particular item may be the first step in driving the demons out of the datebook.

Second, raise questions about *events that are already past.* Looking back, it is possible to assess the importance of commitments, to see what difference attendance at the meeting actually made. It is too late to stop conforming but it is not too early to stop complaining. So you went to the meeting, what difference did it make? How could you have known before the meeting that it didn't/did matter that you were there? How can you know this the next time?

Third, raise questions about a *particular phase of your work.* It may be best to start with a particular *period of the day,* especially a period you do not perceive as a problem. I hear more ministers complain about meetings at night than in the morning or the afternoon. Is this because they think they should have their evenings free? What is the special complaint about evenings?

I also hear a lot of complaints about *office work.* The amount of promotional mail from the denomination is a special scapegoat. What is it about this kind of mail that bothers the pastor? Is it really the amount of it? Does he resent these mailings as "pressure"? Why doesn't he just throw it away? He must either quit complaining or quit conforming if he is to get straight about it.

Pastoral calling comes in for complaints. "I call on a lot of people, but I don't find them at home. This is a waste of time. Why do I have to waste my time this way?" Once again, the commonsense question is the place to begin. Just look at the last five calls you made. How many people were not at home? Really, do you know what percentage of calls you complete? What percentage do you expect to complete? What right have you to expect that your parishioners will be sitting at home waiting for you to call?

B. PASTORAL HIDE-AND-SEEK

Some pastors make a phone call to see if persons are at home before they take the time to visit the house. It is not always necessary to make definite appointments in advance, but there is no reason why the pastor should not do it. Unless he wants to go on playing a popular pastoral game I call "hide-and-seek." This is a game pastors play to keep alive the illusion that they care about people without having to relate to persons.

The rules of the game are very simple. The pastor calls on the homes of people who probably aren't at home. If he has guessed right, he goes to the house at a time when no one is home. He rings the bell or knocks on the door, probably attracting the attention of at least one of the neighbors. Finally, when he realizes (with relief) that no one is home, he celebrates his victory by leaving his calling card—and perhaps by chatting briefly with the neighbor. His joy is complete when the parishioner next sees him, thanks him for stopping by, and says how much the neighbor was impressed with his pastoral concern. In this whole operation, nobody really "meets" anyone. What a marvelous profession we have: we can reach people without touching them! And we convince ourselves that we "love people."

C. NAMING THE DEMONS

Pastors know from their study of the New Testament that you cannot drive out demons unless you know their names. Here are the names of some of the demons that haunt the datebook.

Sleep. Every human being has a basic need to sleep. The pastor must know how much sleep he needs, and plan to get it. Some people must plan to get eight to ten hours of sleep each night or they cannot function. A pastor who knows this about himself must make provision for adequate sleep. Others can survive on five to six hours of sleep. There is nothing virtuous about this. It is one of the personal realities with which the pastor must deal.

Some pastors can get by on five to six hours of sleep a night if, every once in awhile, they can "sleep in" some morning or take a day off. These catch-up periods must be built into the schedule too.

Exercise is another one. I didn't do anything about this for twenty years. Now I am a jogger. I used to consider it was a waste of time to take time in my schedule for exercise. Now I know it is important, and I take the time. In coming to terms with this turning point in my own schedule-building, I became aware of the effect of career changes on all sorts of things, personal as well as professional.

Regularity. Some pastors function well only when they can keep a regular schedule. It is not only "early to bed and early to rise" but "regular to bed and regular to rise" that keeps them going. I find that the older I get the more regular my schedule becomes. This is not so much because I have organized my time well, but because my life has become much more routinized. I have more and better-developed habits now. I recommend an annual audit of time-use and schedule-making to guard against the development of habits that inhibit personal development and professional effectiveness.

Growing old. Schedules must change with changing physical health and vigor. I now know that I cannot function effectively for any extended period of time unless I limit my activity to two out of the three parts of my working day. Leaving the night for sleep, I divide my day into morning, afternoon, and evening. Under normal circumstances, I must keep one of these free from commitments in order to function effectively during the other two.

Local Customs. The pastor has a public role as well as a private life. Ministers differ in their commitments to keeping these separate. But I have discovered that communities differ in the ways in which they evaluate people on an activity-passivity scale. In rural areas I found that most people assumed you were a disciplined and hard-working pastor if you were up and around early in the morning. They didn't care (because they didn't know) if you worked until 3:00 A.M. I also learned that they considered people "lazy" who slept late in the morning. So, lest I be considered "no good," I got into the habit of getting up early in the morning, moving rapidly around the town to make sure I had been seen "up and around," and then going back to bed. In college and seminary I had learned to play the student role. I considered getting up in the morning a sign of stupidity (who wants an eight o'clock class if he can help it!), and studying late at night a sign of scholarship (burning the midnight oil!). I decided that, in the parish, I had to play another game. I called it the "visibility game." And it worked!

Idiosyncrasies. Equal in importance to taking an annual audit of your energy is identifying idiosyncrasies. I discovered something about myself a few years ago that really helped me. I realized that once I had made a commitment and written it in my datebook, I would keep that commitment as a matter of honor. Even if in the meantime I had decided I didn't want to do it and something more important had come up, if I said I would be there, I would be there. So I started making appointments with myself—and keeping them with the same seriousness as my commitments to others. It has been a very helpful move. Being men and not gods, pastors cannot *make* time; they can only take time from what is available. Making appointments with myself is one way I have found to do this.

These little tricks—like setting your watch ahead so you won't be late—are self-deceptions. They are perfectly all right so long as they do not become demonic. Thus, you must "name" the demons you design as well as the ones you discover. Insofar as they help you keep your commitments and pursue your priorities they are justified. They are simply ways of "respecting" yourself, taking yourself seriously. If you are to manage others, you must first manage yourself. *Self-deception* is a dandy device for doing this.

Demythologizing collegiate folklore. Pastoralia is not the only kind of folklore that fouls us up. The folklore of the campus clings for awhile. I remember a piece of campus folk wisdom: "I work best under pressure." Many students would fool around for most of the semester, waiting for that last-minute push before exams when, in a matter of days, they would complete the work of the course, then drop almost dead from exhaustion, mumbling: "I work best under pressure." I know about this, because I used to believe it.

But I had not been out of school a year before I discovered I didn't work *best* under pressure—I worked *only* under pressure. I further discovered that if I didn't put some pressure on myself, somebody else would. If I did not have enough priorities, my parishioners had plenty.

I have still not been able to handle my schedule as well as I would like. I still get boxed in, over-committed, overworked and underemployed. But I have developed some disciplines that help. The most important are the annual audit, making appointments with myself, and getting pastors to talk about their schedules. Every pastor can, and must, tame his time if he is to break out of his passivity. Driving the demons from his datebook is a place to begin.

Blessed is the pastor who tames his time;
he is free from the demons in the datebook.

VI. Developing Professional Disciplines in the Parish

The parish pastor can free himself from captivity to the conform/complaint syndrome through a series of personal moves. But he must also master a repertoire of *professional methods* if he is to maintain his capacity to function effectively in the parish. Many ministers are doing this. Others can learn. But another obstacle emerges in the form of another set of symptoms: the bitch/brag syndrome.

A. THE BITCH/BRAG SYNDROME

When I ask pastors to describe their work, I discover that most of them just can't do it. They can speak in glowing terms about the glories of their calling, the rewards of the ministry, how meaningful their work is. Or they can say how badly it is going, detailing the frustrations and complications they confront. They can say how *good* it is or how *bad* it is, but they can't seem to say *what* it is! This is what I call the bitch/brag syndrome. Just as the conform/complaint syndrome keeps pastors from overcoming their personal passivity, so the bitch/brag syndrome keeps them from seeing their professional responsibility.

If pastors are to develop professional methods that will make them more competent and effective, they must find ways to break out of this syndrome. But first they must understand why they have fallen into it. They wouldn't do it if it didn't help them in some way. What is the problem? What are the symptoms? How does the syndrome function?

B. GLOBAL GOALS AND NITTY-GRITTY

Pastors enter the ministry in response to global goals: building the kingdom, saving souls, helping people, responding to "the call," etc. But in the practice of ministry they find themselves confronted by very specific and concrete situations. The relationship between the global goals and the nitty-gritty of daily procedure is not always clear. How is it that an afternoon visit in the home of a parishioner becomes "pastoral care"? How does a particular sermon become "proclamation of the gospel"? How does presiding at a meeting of the official board become "equipping the saints for ministry"? Beginning with global goals it is hard to make sense of the nitty-gritty.

So the pastor develops a way to deal with the problem. He learns to speak in very positive terms about those things which appear to him meaningful and important (bragging). He also learns a separate language to express his negative feelings about the things he doesn't like, or doesn't do well (bitching). The syndrome expresses his ambivalence about his work. Insofar as the syndrome expresses the reality of his situation it is a good thing. But insofar as it habituates his behavior and inhibits his ability to change it is not a good thing.

One reason why pastors continue to talk this way is that there is a market for it. The pastoral literature consists primarily of bragging (books and articles on the glories and challenges of the calling) and bitching (writing about frustrations, confusions, irrelevancy, and—

finally—"why I left the ministry"). Pastors produce this literature because there is a market for it. It sells.

One thing the literature reveals is a frightening lack of critical discrimination. Pastoral literature tends to be *hypo*-critical—accepting without question every vague romantic notion; or *hyper*-critical—questioning every function, role, and symbol.

This syndrome describes a phenomenon I noted several years ago while studying the changing loyalty patterns of pastors toward denominational programs. I observed that some pastors, who when they were in seminary believed that every denominational program was junk, became staunch promoters of denominational programs soon after they left the seminary. In less than five years the critical seminarian became a responsible pastor, or so it seemed. But on closer investigation (remember my scholarly specialty is preacher-watching) I concluded that the pastor had not changed at all. When he was a "critical seminarian," he appeared to know all about denominational programs and had concluded they were silly. Now that he is a "responsible pastor," he pretends to know all about these programs and concludes they are superior. The one constant in the behavior of the pastor is this: he still has not read most of the literature! He thinks the only options he has are to accept all the programs or to reject all the programs. He has not learned that he must discriminate, employ critical judgment, and make decisions.

The fact is that some denominational programs are pretty good and some are pretty bad. Further, some are better for one situation and worse for another. There is probably some good in all of them and some bad in all of them. The pastor has not been able to discern this because he has not mastered disciplines of discrimination and evaluation. Failing these, he falls into the bitch/brag syndrome and goes merrily on his way.

C. THE SYMPTOMS IN THE SYNDROME

The first steps out of the bitch/brag syndrome are indicated by three simple terms. Each of them reflects a symptom contained in the syndrome and a step on their way out of it. Pastors fall into the bitch/brag syndrome because they do not *respect* their work, have a *regard* for themselves, or *recognize* the consequences of their professional practice.

The first step is *respect*. Most pastors object when I say: "You do not respect your work." But most parish ministers I know just do *not* "respect" their work. In the literal meaning of the word, they do not look back on their actions. That's what the word means: "to respect, to look again." A pastor who does not look back regularly at what he is doing, does not "respect" his work.

The second step is *regard*. This means: "To keep in view, to look closely, to hold in high esteem."

The third step is *recognition*, literally: "to know again, to perceive a thing as previously known."

In these three simple moves a minister gets perspective on his work and finds a way to break the bitch/brag syndrome. But how, specifically, can a pastor do this? I have discovered some things in my preacher-watching that I think can help. As a way of regarding professional activity, I describe the professional event. This comes from "looking closely" at what pastors actually do. As a way of recognizing professional activity, I introduce the case method. This is a way of learning from the practice of ministry. All this is a way of "respecting" the parish ministry—taking it seriously.

Pastors try to develop professional disciplines in many ways. Some steal time for study, seeking in books what may help them to sanity and success. Others leave the parish to attend seminars and workshops, hoping to find new ideas and approaches. These methods are useful, but I prefer an approach that is more like housebreaking a puppy: rubbing their noses in their business until they do it on paper. I am convinced that a rich source of professional learning is immediately accessible to the pastor, if he can only respect it, regard it, and recognize it. What the pastor already knows, but does not recognize, is the place to dig in. But he needs tools with which to dig into the treasures, methods for sorting out the precious materials, and processes for purifying the product. Analyzing the "professional event" is the basic tool. Mastering the use of case material is the major method. And sharing with pastoral colleagues is the primary process. Pastors *can* break the bitch/brag syndrome if they *will*. These methods give the pastor a way to begin.

D. DESCRIBING THE "PROFESSIONAL EVENT"

The "professional event" provides a checklist by which the pastor can study particular aspects of his pastoral work. This helps him identify the professional variables in his practice, and to employ them experimentally. It also allows him to concentrate on special aspects of his work, and to develop them as specialties. Every professional action can be divided into ten distinct "steps." The steps, in turn, take the form of four "stages." The specific nature and duration of each step varies with the particular instance, but the pattern remains the same. By knowing these ten steps and by using them self-consciously, the pastor can keep his bearings and control his actions to maintain professional distance on his practice. I will describe them very briefly, not pausing to illustrate. Pastors will provide the illustrations from their own experience.

Stage One: *Establishing an Appropriate Relationship,* *(Perception, Recognition, Responsibility)*

1. *Perception.* This is the simple experience of being aware that there is something or someone before you. It may be a person or a problem. A person appears. He wants to "see" you. The first act in the professional event is to "see" the person.

One of the problems in our society is that persons in need have difficulty getting the attention of the professional who can serve them. I believe there are many people who have some need who do not know what ails them or what anyone can do about it. When they hurt badly enough they will seek help, usually turning to the most visible, available, and accessible professional. Many of these people will turn to a pastor, not because they have a "religious problem" or because they see themselves as "religious people." They need help and do not know where to turn. Later on I will describe a specialized pastoral ministry for the parish clergyman, designed as a response to this problem.

2. *Recognition.* The second step in the professional event often requires the correction of initial perceptions. This is the literal meaning of the word: to see again. Critical at this point is the pastor's ability to see things from the perspective of the person or persons involved. Even if he decides that the person does not understand his own problem, he must be able to see how the other perceives and recognizes his own situation.

3. *Responsibility.* Having perceived the problem and recognized it for what it is, the pastor must now make his first decision. Is this a problem for me, am I responsible? The answer to this question defines the relationship the professional will establish with the person. The pastor

uses two guidelines for deciding about responsibility: ecclesiastical and professional.

(a) Ecclesiastical responsibility is implied for members of the parish. Whether or not the pastor is professionally competent to deal with the situation, he has
a formal responsibility toward his parishioners. He is
required by custom, and often by his own commitments,
to accept responsibility for the pastoral care of those who
are part of the parish.

(b) Professional responsibility is indicated when the
problem is "religious" in some respect, or when the
pastor has the special professional competence to deal
with it.

These two guidelines assist the pastor to make a preliminary decision about his responsibility. He has three
alternatives.

(1) He may *accept* responsibility for the person and
his problem. Later on he may decide to reject or refer
but, for the time being, he accepts professional responsibility and establishes a pastoral relationship.

(2) He may *refer* responsibility, either to another
pastor or to another professional. Sometimes the referral
is temporary, as to a specialist with provision for the
person to return. In other cases it may be a permanent
referral.

(3) He may *reject* responsibility by turning the person away with no provision for a relationship or referral.
This is sometimes an appropriate action. It is difficult
for the pastor and so he seldom does it. But it remains a
formal option at this stage of the professional event.

The difference between these actions is not always
crystal clear, but three distinct options are always present, and the pastor must clarify the terms under which
he is acting in order to be truly responsible.

Each profession has a characteristic "language of responsibility." When a doctor says, "This man is sick," he is saying, "This is my kind of problem." If he says, "There is nothing physically wrong with you," he is saying, "I cannot assume responsibility for you." One of the questions always before the pastor is: what are the situations and conditions for which I am responsible? Without some clarity about the purpose of the ministry this kind of question cannot be answered. But, with or without clarity, the pastor is "in the act" when he assumes any kind of responsibility.

Stage Two: *Preparing for Action (Diagnosis, Design, Decision)*

4. *Diagnosis.* Using his professional training and skill the pastor seeks to understand in more depth and detail the nature of the problem before him. He brings into play the whole range of his professional competence, and using the skills and knowledge at his disposal, he seeks to understand the person and his problem.

5. *Design of alternatives.* Having decided the nature of the problem, he now considers alternative strategies for dealing with it. He considers his own competence, the resources at his disposal, and his ability to respond in light of his other responsibilities. He tries to answer the question: what is best for this person? He considers his alternatives, inventing new approaches as he is able to do so, as well as using standard strategies that are immediately available.

6. *Decision.* Now the question is: what will *I* do? At this point he may choose to redefine his relationship, temporarily returning to Step 3, rejecting or referring responsibility. He may, in effect, refer the person to himself, having decided that he is the most qualified available professional. In this case he decides to work with the per-

son toward the resolution of his difficulty. But he still has not acted decisively. He must still do something. That is the next step. From the alternatives available to him he has selected the one which, in his professional judgment, is the best. It remains to be seen if he is right!

Stage Three: *The Heart of the Matter (Action)*

7. *Action.* The professional now acts on the basis of his decision. He does what he has decided to do. Whether it is a simple, brief, and decisive act or a long, complicated, and indeterminate one, it is the heart of the professional event. It is the thing he does. During this stage he may correct perceptions, revise diagnoses, design new alternatives, employing the disciplines appropriate to these other steps in the event.

Stage Four: *Learning from the Event (Description, Analysis, Evaluation)*

After the action, the professional continues to exercise professional responsibility through disciplined procedures of description, analysis, and evaluation. They follow the action, but are part of the total professional event. Critical to the final stage of the act is the keeping of records. Without a clear, accurate, and complete record of the total event, the pastor cannot sustain his professional activity. I will say more about record-keeping in a moment.

8. *Description.* The professional now describes what has taken place in the event. He does this primarily for himself, to have a record of the event. It is a way in which the professional can get a picture of himself in action, a kind of mirror held up in which he is reflected to himself. This is not easy to do, but it can be done. The case method, which I will describe in the next chapter is one way to learn.

9. *Analysis.* The professional is not yet prepared to pass judgment on his performance. He must first analyze his actions. As in Step 4 he sought to diagnose the person's problem, so now he seeks to understand his professional actions. He moves through each of the steps. What did I see? What do I see now that I did not see then? Could I have seen it at that time? If not, why not? What responsibility did I accept? What, really, was my diagnosis? What alternatives did I design? Were there others I might have considered? What was my activity after selecting an alternative? What has been the result of my actions? Did I do something I have never done before? Did I improvise or innovate? What did I learn that was new to me? Did I confirm some things I already knew?

10. *Evaluation.* The final step in the event is made easier by careful description and analysis. The pastor can evaluate his performance in the two ways I will describe in more detail in relation to the case method: professional competence and theological adequacy.

E. ONE EVENT AFTER ANOTHER

By now the pastor is involved in another professional event—and has been involved in several at the same time. He has been preparing sermons, organizing activities, attending meetings, conducting funerals, etc. No pastor *works* at one thing at a time. But it is possible for him to *focus* on one thing at a time, to select it out for special attention. By doing this the pastor develops the discipline of "professional distance," freeing himself from the tyranny of the torrent of crises and emergencies that tend to frustrate him, and the round of routine duties that tend to bore him. As he develops his ability to describe, analyze, and evaluate professional events, he develops a professional method that can help him move beyond professionalism to deeper dimensions of ministry.

I have described the professional event in terms of the individual pastor. This makes it clear that a pastor can develop disciplines by himself. But professional self-development is aided by colleagues who share common concerns and are devoted to common disciplines. The perspective of professional colleagues is critical to the development of professional distance. For this reason I want to describe in some detail a "case method" I have developed through which groups of ministers can work together toward mutual professional development. An understanding of the professional event illuminates the nature of "case material." Therefore I have discussed it first.

As you read on, you will see that the structure of the professional act provides the outline for the case material which pastors can use to develop a "case method" for professional self-development. The first two stages, comprising six steps, provide material for the "background." The "description" in the case is based on the records of the action (Step 7) developed in Step 8. "Analysis" and "evaluation" in the case correspond to those parts of the event.

Both in the discussion of the professional event and the case method I have concentrated on issues involving individuals. The same method can be used for social problems and issues. Here are some sample cases to show how events of both sorts can be used as case material.

SAMPLE CASE #1

BACKGROUND: My church is located in a "bedroom community" of about 5,000 highly trained technicians and engineers in a population center of over 100,000. Most of the people who have joined our new church are young couples with small children. We had no young people beyond 9th grade, and only four in the 9th grade. My attempts to get acquainted with young people in the community were met with suspicion and hostility at first, but we got a small group started. Youth meetings were structured largely by the group, my method being to get acquainted first, then begin to structure the group after they had confidence in me.

Chris is a 15-year-old 9th-grader I have tried to involve in our church and youth group. His parents are sensitive, hard-working, intelligent people of culture and refinement. They enjoy their home and their work. They have no TV in their home—they can't be bothered with such trivia. Chris has two older brothers—one in the Peace Corps and the other in the university. Chris did not want to attend our bi-weekly meetings but came at the insistence of his parents.

At one of these meetings, the person with the program did not come at the last minute, and the group decided to talk about drugs. Without any advance preparation Chris gave what amounted to a lecture which covered such things as the origin of marijuana, heroin, and LSD, the chemical analysis of each, the physiological effects on the body, etc. He did this with the competence of a college professor explaining it to group of laymen.

DESCRIPTION: One evening not long after this I called at Chris's home. His parents were away, and he was studying. He invited me in. He told me he was reading Dante's *Inferno* in research for an assigned composition which was "to select some historical character you believe has gone to hell and tell why you think so." In the conversation that followed Chris told me he had read extensively in science, philosophy, and current literature—

and that he did not believe in the existence of God. I tried to suggest he might not have all the evidence yet to make such a decision; that many scientists believe in God. I was inclined to accept his statements as evidence of one who had given considerable thought to them.

ANALYSIS: I was so overwhelmed with this boy's knowledge and his probing mind which was questioning the things I didn't until my college days that I "froze." I felt it was obvious to him I had little to offer to challenge him at his intellectual level. He is an exceptional boy, but I have discovered that many young people in this community are not far behind.

EVALUATION: 1. How do I minister to young people like this?

2. How can I prepare myself to handle situations where my incompetence in science and technology is so obvious?

3. How can I handle the "freeze" situations?

SAMPLE CASE #2

BACKGROUND: As in most denominations presently there is a great amount of tension arising from different understandings of the nature and mission of the church. Within our denomination there is a divisive group, composed mainly of laymen who have been circularizing the church and seeking to sow seeds of ill will and dissension, particularly in setting laymen over against the ministers. I heard of an organization meeting of this group in our city and decided to attend the meeting even though it was really intended for laymen only. Five of the members of our church were there. It upset me greatly that this divisive group might get a foothold in this church. In the weeks that followed all the officers received information though the mail from this group, with attacks and insinuations about the subversion of the church. I determined that I would have to do something about this in a meeting of the officers.

EVENT: I chose to speak on this at the next monthly meeting of one of the boards. During the meeting some of the men made charges about the denomination which had obviously come from this dissident group. They alluded to the stand on social issues, control of church property, and the lack of value of the church magazine. Much to my surprise, some of the men who support the church wholeheartedly were mute that evening. I felt very much alone as I tried to answer some of these unfounded attacks. At the end of the meeting it was customary for me to speak to the group about any matter that concerned me. I talked about this dissident group and their insinuations about the leadership of the church. I maintained that such a group in the church was more of a problem than a solution, and stated that if we were more faithful in seeking guidance from God's Word we would have a better and more effective church. Finally I told them that I disagreed with them and disapproved of this group, and it was my responsibility as their pastor to tell them how I felt.

ANALYSIS: I am sure that my speech alienated some of the men at the meeting, at least for a time, I was really very threatened by the discussion that had taken place, and even though my personal security in the church was not threatened I took it very personally. I was very defensive, and later realized that I had manipulated them emotionally at the very time that I was denying any manipulation. My advice about more use of the Word of

God was a smoke screen, because I had not used the Bible in the meeting any more than they.

EVALUATION: I was not every effective in combatting the attitudes of some of those officers because of my defensiveness. I do feel that I had to take some stand for the sake of those who did not understand it. The one good thing that emerged was that they expressed gratitude that I told them how I felt, even though they may have disagreed. I need to learn how to deal more effectively with hostility and opposition. How might I have handled the problem more effectively?

VII. A Case Method for Pastors

This chapter is a description of the particular case method I have developed. By doing this I do not mean to imply that this is the best form of the case method, nor that the case method is the only one. This is simply what I know best. And, in the manner of the case method, I will take time to tell the story of how I stumbled into it, how it has developed, and what I have learned through the use of it with both seminary students and parish clergy. I have included the text of some material I have prepared to orient actual groups of pastors to the use of the method, along with some cases. What follows, then, is designed to enable groups of pastors to begin to use the case method.

A. I DISCOVER THE CASE METHOD

My own use of the case method grew out of my need to find a way to supervise the field education of students at Vanderbilt Divinity School. I did not have the time, the energy, or the training to do much personal supervision "in the field." I needed to find a way to work with students at my convenience on campus, rather than at their convenience in the field. I began by organizing "field education seminars." The seminars met for one hour each week and consisted of small groups of students who were at work in a variety of field settings. The students seemed to enjoy and profit from these informal opportunities for discussion each week. I found them invaluable as a way of keeping in touch with what students were facing in the field and how they were relating these experiences to their studies in the seminary.

But very early I became aware that the sessions were not uniformly helpful, either to me or to the students. Some days we would spend an hour listening to one of the students tell about a problem he faced in his parish. At the end of the hour the student felt better for having "talked it out" with his peers, and the others felt that they had been "helpful." But the hour was over before the issues were focused for the group, and there was little opportunity for careful analysis or serious evaluation. I began the search for a style of seminar which would be open on one end to the emerging experiences of students in the field, and open on the other end to their structured life of learning in the seminary. What I needed was a device to focus the work of the seminar on concrete cases, although at the time I did not know how to develop such a device.

B. THE IDEA OF THE "EVENT"

It appeared to me that the basic problem in getting at issues lay in the fact that the discussions in the seminars tended to alternate between *anecdotes* on the one hand (detailed, concrete, personal reports that were not really open to the perception of the group) and *abstractions* on the other hand (general ideas about ministry, programs, doctrines). What was needed, therefore, was a way to present concrete instances of practice to a group of peers for purposes of learning. The possibility of a "case study" of an "event" commended itself. I used the term "event" because it was a neutral term, making clear that I wanted descriptions not of "problems" or "issues" or "failures" or "successes," but of a piece of practice which could be presented to the seminar for analysis and evaluation.

An event is, by definition, an occasion in which the professional acts as a responsible agent. (See details above, Chapter VI, pp. 73-78.) It is not a happening he observes, but an event in which he participates. A report of this event, then, will reveal the character of his involvement, his commitment, and his competence. By requiring students to write cases out of their own involvement, I meant to suggest that they were, themselves, involved in situations of some importance and that they could learn from reflection on their own activities.

C. WRITING THE CASE

Because of the limitations under which I began to work (a small group of relatively inexperienced students who met for only one hour each week to discuss their field experience), I developed a form of case writing and a discipline for discussing them under those limitations. I have continued to use the same form with groups of parish clergy. Here is the memorandum I prepared to describe the discipline of case-writing. It is sent to pastors, along with sample cases, to guide their preparation for a "case conference."

Memorandum to Ministers

The case conference is based on case material prepared by the ministers who participate. I set the *structure*. You provide the *content*. The structure provides a method for getting hold of issues in practice. The cases provide both the content and context of the issues. We do not discuss "subjects" or "issues" or "problems" in the abstract. We deal with cases—accounts of events in ministerial practice. When we meet for the case conference we will "get down to cases." But first we must have the cases.

1. The case must be written: A "case" is a written report of an *event* in which you were involved as a minister with some responsibility for the outcome. The purpose of writing the case is to produce a record of the event.

2. The written case must be brief: The case report is to be written on one side of a single sheet of paper—no longer. Part of the discipline is to learn what can be condensed into this limited space. Limitations of space force the writer to identify critical information.

3. The case must have four parts: The four parts are to be clearly distinguished. They need not be equal in length. But each of the parts must be included, or the case cannot be discussed at the conference.

(a) *Background:* enough information to set the event in context. What you had in mind, what you hoped/feared would happen, when and how you became aware of/involved in the event, what pressures and persons precipitated and shaped the event.

(b) *Description:* what happened and what you did. Report the event, including as much detail as possible in the limited space.

(c) *Analysis:* identify issues and relationships, with special attention to changes and resistance to change. Try to answer the question: What's going on here?

(d) *Evaluation:* your estimate of your own effectiveness in the event. Did you do what you set out to do? Did you function effectively? If so, why so? If not, why not? What factors or forces emerged which you did not anticipate? What questions might the group discuss that would be most helpful to you?

4. Clarify the question of confidentiality: If you do not want to reveal the identity of persons and institutions, use fictitious names and addresses (Mrs. A, Mr. B, X Church, Y town). If you reveal identity, but wish the information to be confidential in the group, write at the top: "CONFIDENTIAL: For conference use only."

D. THE CASE CONFERENCE

Cases become the subject matter for tightly structured seminar sessions in which (a) a *group* of ministers or seminary students (b) assume clearly defined *roles* (c) for the discussion of a specific case according to a strict *docket*. The design of the case conference, like the form of the written case, grew out of the limitations under which I began to develop my own case method. I continue to use it with various kinds of groups, partly because I am familiar with it, and partly to test one very limited method under a variety of conditions.

(a) The *group* may vary in size from three to twelve persons. I prefer a group of six to ten, because of the strict limits of time under which I choose to work. My objectives in using a group are: to help them discover the resources for professional self-education that exist in the group, to help them learn that they can learn from one another, and to help them grow in their ability to trust their colleagues to assist them in improving their professional competence. Members of the group may vary widely in age, experience, and ability. It does not seem to matter much whether they are similar in denomination, training, or professional status. In fact, one of the discoveries in every group is the "variety of gifts" in the group.

(b) Three clearly distinguished *roles* are played by members of the group.

The "presenter" has written the case and has distributed it to members of the group in advance of the seminar.

The "discussants" have received their copies in advance and are required to spend at least one hour in studying the case.

The "leader" has consulted with the presenter,

helped him to write his case, and is responsible for the conduct of the case conference.

(c) The case conference follows a strict *docket*, which controls the time allowed for each part of the discussion, and allows for the assumption of appropriate roles by members of the group. In the following description I have shown the time docketed, the roles played, and the tasks of the group at each point in the discussion.

Time: 5 *minutes*. Task: *Clarification of information*

The group may ask the presenter questions of information. The leader firmly resists attempts of the group to begin analysis or evaluation. The point is to provide an occasion for members of the group, on the basis of their study of the case, to ask for additional information and clarification. One of the critical questions for the professional is to learn what he needs to know in order to do what he has to do. This part of the docket forces the group to discriminate between information that is interesting and information that is critical. The leader stops the questioning after five minutes and turns the group to its next task.

Time: 25 *minutes*. Task: *Analysis of dynamics in event*

The presenter becomes timekeeper for the group and cannot participate actively in the discussion. This is, of course, frustrating to him. He thinks of all sorts of things he should have put in the case. The group wants to ask further questions. This is ruled out by the leader as the group concentrates on analysis. The main function of the leader is to guide the discussion, keeping the group from jumping too quickly to evaluation, and forcing them to clarify their understanding of the dynamics of the event.

I often use a technique I call "unfolding the event": a quick recapitulation of the "description" after clarifying the important background factors. The task of the discussants at this point is to clarify the issues, identify turning points and critical factors, and to lay the foundation for serious evaluation. At the end of twenty-five minutes it is the task of the presenter to call "time," and the leader turns the group to evaluation.

Time: *10 minutes.* Task: *Evaluation of performance*

The leader now presses the discussants to make professional evaluations of the practice of the presenter. The evaluation has two parts. The first task is to evaluate professional competence. The basic questions are: Did this man do what he set out to do? How well did he do it? What, if anything, could he have done that would have made any difference? If the man offered any self-evaluation in the written case, we begin with his own evaluation. This forces a man to clarify his objectives, and in writing future cases, to state them. If a man doesn't know what he set out to do, he will never know what he has accomplished! The second task is to assess theological adequacy. The critical questions are: Was this worth doing, or was it worth all the time and effort it took to do it? At this point theological norms, historical traditions, social needs, etc. become critical. What is at stake is the adequacy of the action in relation to the nature of the church, the meaning of ministry, the hierarchy of needs and values of persons and society. The group might decide that the man did a beautiful job, accomplishing what he set out to do, but that the task was not necessary, or valid, or worth the time and effort it took. Here the conflicting demands on the clergyman are sorted out, a man's priorities are called into question or confirmed, and the group seeks to help the man clarify the nature of his professional commitment. The presenter again performs his task as timekeeper and calls the group to the next item on the docket.

Time: *10 minutes.* **Task:** *Reflection and reaction by presenter*

The presenter now has opportunity to feedback to the group and to respond to their discussion. I suggest the following questions: At what points was the analysis and evaluation of the group most helpful? What has the group still failed to see and understand? What questions would he like the group to address if it had more time?

Time: *10-minute break before the next case*

The leader declares the session adjourned. If the group is discussing several cases at a case conference, he will call them back together at the end of the break, introduce the next presenter, and begin the discussion of another case according to the docket. Thus, in a one-hour period, concentrating on a one-page case, a group of from three to twelve ministers address an event in professional practice under this form of the case method.

This much information should give a group enough to get started. But for those who want to know more about the method, availability of case material, and other uses of the case method, further details are given in the next chapter. Additional cases are in the appendix.

VIII. More on the Case Method

My efforts to promote the case method among pastors have met with a gratifying response. After working with a number of case conference groups in Alabama, Tennessee, New York, and Florida, I have been able to establish a Case Method Project at Lancaster Theological Seminary. Under the leadership of the Reverend Arthur Sherman, this project is training ministers in the use of the method, developing case material and training instruments, and organizing a network of pastors to staff the growing project. In addition, members of the Academy of Parish Clergy have been using the case-group model as a means of managing their own continuing education and professional development. Most of the material in these two sections on the case method appeared in the first issue of the *Journal of the Academy of Parish Clergy,* and groups of ministers in several communities have used the material as a manual to begin their own groups.

Others have been working at developing the case method in other ways and in other places. Under a grant from the Sealantic Foundation, the American Association of Theological Schools is sponsoring a Case Study Institute that coordinates the resources of the Boston Theological Institute and the Harvard Business School in a three-year pilot project. Professor Keith Bridston will direct the project, which is designed primarily to develop the use of the case method for theological education in the seminaries. It may be that the use of the case method will be

a major instrument for the reform of theological education, as well as for the professional development of ministers. That will be good.

A. WHAT MAKES A GOOD CASE?

Writing a good case is not easy. Very few pastors can
do it the first time they try, but almost all can learn
quickly. I have discovered that the following elements
tend to make a good case.

1. Clearly stated objectives. If a man does not know
what he was trying to do, he will never know whether he
did it or not. And if he does not project some performance
goals for himself, he has no basis for evaluating his effectiveness. Some pastors find it hard to state their goals and
objectives, partly because they sound so puny. But the
alternative is to go with global goals, which are no help
at all. The case forces the writer to identify his professional objectives. He must either state them, or admit that
he did not have any in this case.

2. A point of decision between alternatives. Decision-
making is the heart of professional practice. A case in
which there is no "turning point" is not very useful—at
least for the purposes for which I use cases. I am trying
to get at the dynamics of parish practice, using professional models as a guide. I have tried to make the point
earlier that the characteristic of a "professional event" is
one in which a decision is required. A case that does not
focus on a decision-action event may be an interesting
account of an occasion, but it is not a description of an
event—and therefore is not a good case.

3. Sufficient critical information. Many cases include
irrelevant or unimportant data—even when the pastor is
allowed only one page on which to write his case! Part
of the discipline in case-writing is to distinguish the im-

portant from the merely interesting. A case may neglect to report that the woman was crying when she came into the study, or that the pastor was scared to death, or that the vote in the official board, reported as a "crushing defeat" for the pastor, was really 5 to 4! By compressing the case onto one page, the pastor is encouraged to separate out irrelevent data. This, in itself, is a useful discipline.

4. An event in which several options were present. The purpose of a case is not to prove a point or illustrate an ideal solution to a problem. The purpose is to picture the event "in motion," as it happened, complete with the perceptions and reactions of the pastor. Seldom does a case conference agree on the "right" solution, but in a fruitful discussion of a well-written case, the alternatives can be identified and the nature of the decision clarified. Only when this can be done is significant analysis and evaluation possible.

B. SOURCES OF CASE MATERIAL

(1) The two main sources of cases are those already in print and those produced by members of case conference groups. I prefer to use cases produced by members of the group, for three reasons.

First, case-writing is a very valuable professional discipline. It is one method ministers can use to design their practice for professional development. Most ministers discover that case-writing is its own reward. Just writing up a piece of practice is a way of getting hold of it so it can be described, analyzed, and evaluated. It is a way of "respecting" one's work. Most ministers want to be more professional in their practice, but just don't know how. Writing cases is a way to get started. I have been delighted to discover that some ministers who have been introduced to the case method in case conference groups now write a case each week as a private professional discipline.

Second, the case method provides a basis for professional relationships among pastors. Ministers often complain that theirs is a "lonely profession," that ministers don't trust one another, that ministers can't help one another—but don't do anything about it (the conform/complaint syndrome). In case conference groups ministers learn not only *that* they can trust one another, but *how* they can learn from one another. The method provides a kind of neutral ground on which pastors can gather. A pastor does not have to reveal anything about his work which he wishes to conceal. No one tells him what he must write up as a case, only that he must do it. He can pick some event that shows him in a good light or a bad light, which he considers a success or a failure. He can write up an event that he considers trivial and ordinary, or one that he considers critical or extraordinary.

I expect to see more groups of pastors using the case method, perhaps organized as local units of the Academy of Parish Clergy. In this way ministers can move toward professional collegiality on their own initiative. They do not have to wait for someone to organize them. They can concentrate on special facets of parish practice, like family counseling, conflict situations, youth problems, etc. Or they can deal with the whole range of events in pastoral practice. I have encouraged groups to try a variety of approaches. Whichever way they go they have a concrete method for relating professionally.

A third reason I prefer to use cases produced by pastors, rather than those already in print, is my own need for this material. As a seminary professor who tries to prepare students for the practice of ministry, I need the cases written by pastors. Without them I cannot confront my students with the realities of the profession as it is being practiced today. I must either draw on my memory, recalling events from over fifteen years ago, or I must rely on printed material. As I have said before, most of the writing about the parish is done by the wrong people. It is done by seminary professors who really don't know what is going on or by ministerial dropouts who really don't care. I want for my students the best firsthand accounts available. I find that cases written by-pastors are the best source.

And beyond my own personal need for this information is the need of the profession for a literature. This literature is critical to the development of a pastoral theology based on the realities of the profession. The best single source of information about the practice of ministry is the practitioners. One way to get that information into public view is for pastors to write cases. The one-page case is only a beginning, as is the fifty-minute case conference. From these simple beginnings we can learn how to build a more adequate data-base and develop more sophisticated methods for the description, analysis, and evaluation of parish practice. Cases now in print illustrate the emergence of this literature.

(2) Some cases in print are available, and more are being produced as the case method gains in popularity and usefulness. Those interested in the kind of case material I have been describing should write to the Case Method Project, Lancaster Theological Seminary, Lancaster, Pa. 17603. Sample cases along with instructions for their use in case conference groups and workshops are available upon request. Here are some other cases I have found interesting and useful.

Grace Ann Goodman has for several years written case studies for the Institute of Strategic Studies of the United Presbyterian Board of National Missions. Some of the best are gathered into a volume entitled *Rocking the Ark,* available from the Board at 475 Riverside Drive, New York, New York 10027.

Harold Fray has written a case study of his own parish as it passed through a major crisis. Published as *Conflict and Change in the Church* (Pilgrim Press, 1969) this is one of the best illustrations of the kind of pastoral literature for which I am calling.

The Society for the Advancement of Education for Ministry (SACEM) has sponsored the writing of several cases. These are available from the Society, 3401 Brook Road, Richmond, Virginia 23227.

The Harvard Business School has prepared at least one very interesting case called *Westfield Church.* It comes in two parts and is available from the Intercollegiate Case Clearing House, Soldiers Field Post Office, Boston, Massachusetts 02163.

Some of the traditional pastoral literature can be used as "case" material, but much of it has the quality of "pastoralia." Even the best, like Bernanos' *Diary of a Country Priest,* is heavily anecdotal, tending to tell stories to illustrate points rather than to describe events. Such autobiographical statements can be useful when they describe events in enough detail to provide a basis for professional analysis and evaluation. Reinhold Niebuhr's little classic *Leaves From the Notebook of a Tamed Cynic* has helped me convince some seminarians that the discipline of case writing can be theologically respectable!

C. WHAT MAKES A GOOD CASE CONFERENCE GROUP?

It is hard to have a good case conference discussion without a good case, but a good group can get a lot out of a bad case if they are skillful. I will report some things I have discovered about the nature of case groups, and some of the analytical devices which seem to facilitate productive discussion.

I have already commented on the size of the group. I prefer a group of about eight, although I can work with from three to fifteen. Using the strict docket as a point of departure, a group of more than ten is often frustrated by the shortness of time. If only twenty-five minutes are allowed for analysis and there are twelve in the group, that means only about two minutes per man. And what preacher can say much in two minutes!

The composition of the group is relatively unimportant, I have discovered. The case method is a great leveler. What counts in the group is professional competence. It doesn't matter what the pastor's education, denomination, size of church. If he can see the issues, articulate the alternatives, and communicate effectively with his peers, he can function well in the group. I have worked with groups that spanned the generation gap, embraced the theological spectrum, ran the denominational gamut, and included the whole range of geographical locations from ghetto to mountain outpost. I have also worked with homogeneous groups, pastors from the same locality, and even the same seminary! After the first two cases, these differences disappear and the professional expertise begins to appear. The semi-literate country preacher points out to the pastor with the Ph.D. some things that are helpful. The young minister instructs the older man, and the high-steeple pastor contributes helpful perspectives on rural realities. This is one reason why I am so enthusiastic about the case method as a strategy for building the Academy of Parish Clergy. It provides a truly professional basis upon which to establish collegial relationships, and it can support and develop these relationships.

It makes a difference to have the "presenter" present. Some pastors feel that the group can be more objective about a case written by someone who is not a member of the group. I have had a chance to test this in several groups. It is often necessary to use a sample case to get a particular group organized. In this way the group has an opportunity to experience the difference it makes to have the presenter present. The first thing they realize is that their basic source of information is missing. They cannot ask the presenter for additional information. And, at the end, they get no feedback from the man whose case they have been discussing.

Then, when they turn to cases written by members of the group, they begin to see the difference. The man who has written the case is present during the discussion. What they are saying is being heard by him, so he can profit from their professional judgment. The group begins to feel that they are contributing something to him. It gives a sense of reality and importance to the proceedings. And the docket gives the presenter the last word. He will evaluate the evaluators!

Evidently some pastors remember those practice-preaching sessions in seminary in which the poor student-preacher is cut to ribbons by both professor and students. They fear the repetition of that kind of experience. What they discover in the case conference is that they have become pastors. They can deal professionally with their peers. There are no outside experts present, no professor to grade them. There is no competition, no need to "pass." A kind of "pastoral care" is present. And they tend to lose their concern to be "objective" as they see they are dealing with one another.

Since I am trying to help pastors toward autonomy, the most important characteristic of the group is their willingness to assume responsibility for themselves. I will not normally work with a group that does not intend to become self-sustaining. Therefore, I move a group into leadership roles as quickly as possible. I have found that, after leading the group myself through from three to six cases, the group can run itself.

D. WHAT METHODS HELP THE GROUP DEVELOP SKILL IN DISCUSSION?

Five general patterns emerge as the group becomes more skillful in discussing cases.

1. The resources in the group begin to emerge. One pastor becomes the "resident expert" on money matters, another on youth problems, another on liturgical forms, and another on organization and management. Personal styles also emerge. One man communicates by asking sharp questions, another provides the humor that keeps the discussion moving, another has theories about things and can conceptualize helpfully.

2. Categories and concepts emerge that help the group in analyzing and evaluating the case. Each group must attack this problem for itself. Pastors have not learned a common language to use in professional discussion. For instance, it takes awhile for the denominational lingo to surface and submerge again, and we have a need in the profession for functional concepts that illuminate pastoral events.

I have spoken unkindly about "pastoralia." Now I want to say a good word for it. I think there are real possibilities in the use of "preacher talk" when it is subjected to the disciplines of group process. I have found that some pastors can use a kind of homiletical imagery to open up the dynamics of pastoral practice.

I was working with a group of pastors in Alabama, using the case method to get at conflict management. One member of the group started to play around with nautical imagery in the manner of a preacher thinking about a ser-

mon. He didn't know much about ships, but he was trying. (It was like Paul talking about a grain of wheat
falling into the ground and dying. Paul didn't know much
about agriculture, but he was trying to make a point the
the best way he could. We all know that if a seed falls
into the ground and dies, it is just plain dead. Paul didn't
know that, but he made his point.) At any rate, this
brother was saying something like this:

You know, it is kind of like when you are sailing—or at least
what I hear about sailing—that on a clear day when the wind
is behind you, you can just run up your sail, point the ship
in the direction you want to go, and sail. Some people call
that "smooth sailing." But some days the wind doesn't blow.
What do you do in a sailboat when there is no wind? Then
there are days when the wind is not behind you, but is blowing
right at you. What do you do then? You have to "tack" into
the wind. You go first to the right, and then to the left. If you
don't know about sailing, you could look at a fellow doing
this and get the idea that he didn't know where he was going.
But if he's a good sailor, he knows where he is going, and he
knows what he has to do to get there. He will tack back and
forth across the wind many times to get where he wants to go.
Then there are other times when the wind is so bad and the
sea is so rough that all you can do is to pull down your sail,
batten down the hatches, and hang on! [He was speaking
about an experience he had just been through the week before.]

Now this may sound pretty simple-minded to those interested in "pure research." But I would argue that this
pastor had developed a fairly sophisticated typology of
conflict situations. And he did it using homiletical images.
I have found that a good way to get pastors thinking about
their work professionally is to encourage them to use the
categories and concepts with which they are familiar. Although homiletical imagery is not always precise, it is

one of the analytical tools which pastors have. We need
to expore ways in which it can become more professionally
responsible.

3. Strategies for getting into cases and at the issues begin to emerge. I have mentioned "unfolding the event."
This is a simple move by which a member of the group
tries to restate the event in his own words. The purpose is
to open up the dynamics of the event, to show the turning points.

Another device is to measure the degree of freedom the
pastor has in the situation. Did he choose to participate
in this event? Was he free not to get involved? Was he
caught, trapped, or otherwise surprised by the event? Cases
can be categorized on a scale from active to passive at this
point. It makes a difference whether the event was a crisis
in which the pastor was caught or a program that the
pastor had planned.

It is also helpful to make explicit the "projective" quality of the case method. Pastors will identify with partici-
pants in the event. They will tend to "take sides" for or
against the pastor in the case. This is a factor that the
discussion leader will use to help members of the group
see themselves more clearly. If a member of the group
keeps referring to a particular person or action in the case
it is often an indication that he is seeing himself in the
case at that point.

Revealing language in the written case provides a clue
to the issues and dynamics. When the pastor reports that
he was "surprised" or "angry" his feelings are showing.
When the language of polarization appears (I-them, we-
they) there is another clue to follow.

As the group becomes experienced in the method, and
familiar with the special resources and skills in the group,
methods begin to be used self-consciously by the group.
A member of the group may say: "Let's unfold the event."

This is a sign that he has learned to use that method self-consciously.

4. Theological method begins to develop. This is, of course, my primary interest. I want to develop the case method as a discipline for "doing theology" in the parish. I find pastors begin first to use the "doctrine of the ministry" as a theological category. "Who does this fellow think he is, doing a thing like that?" becomes "What concept of ministry does he have?" Next, notions of the church become functional. "He has a curious idea of what the church is" becomes "He seems to be saying he believes in the priesthood of believers, but he doesn't act like it."

In the evaluation of the case, after trying to measure professional competence, we press for questions of theological adequacy. At this point the leader has the hardest job. He must press, finally, the question: how is God at work in this case? I have been delighted to see pastors who were at first embarrassed by this question, begin to address it. After all, the purpose of the case method is to analyze not just psychologically and sociologically, but also theologically. In the end we must ask: What does this say about man before God?

5. The group begins to develop its own style of work. One of the first signs that the group has begun to function professionally is when they decide to change the docket. I begin with a very strict discipline of the docket, stopping each period abruptly and moving decisively to the next. But once the group has been through a number of cases they begin to sense when they have about completed the analysis, and someone suggests that we move to evaluation. Or, on the other hand, when the analysis is not really completed in the allotted time, the group may decide to extend the docket and take some more time for analysis before moving to evaluation.

I have discovered that pastors respond very readily to a

direct and disciplined approach. Usually before the second case has been discussed some member will intervene during the analysis with the comment: "I guess this is not really analysis, but evaluation." My strategy is to say: "Go ahead and try; I'll let you know if it is appropriate." In this way the group becomes aware of the differences between analysis and evaluation—and within the evaluation, to distinguish between professional and theological norms.

In these and other ways I have been encouraged by my use of the case method. Most ministers respond readily to the opportunity to relate professionally to their colleagues. They catch on quickly to the disciplines of the method and begin to develop their own. By the time members of the group begin to assume the "leader" role, they are well on their way to professional autonomy. They are also beginning to believe in themselves and to respect their work.

E. SOME OTHER USES FOR THE CASE METHOD

Pastors who have been introduced to the case method in groups of ministers report that they find the method useful in a variety of ways in their local parishes. One pastor has used it with study groups wrestling with ethical issues. Members of the group are asked to write up events in which they faced moral decisions. These cases are used as a basis for group discussions. Another pastor has used the method to train teachers for the church school. One pastor has used it in marriage counseling. He asks a couple having trouble to write up an event in which they both participated. Each writes his own case, and then they compare cases. He finds the method helps them to see some of the sources of their differences.

These kinds of reports encourage me about the possibility of new and different uses of the method. They also illustrate the essentially "neutral" quality of the method. No one is asked to report anything he does not want to reveal. In writing the case, the writer evaluates himself according to his own criteria. There is no right or wrong thing to report, no good or bad way to act. The method, therefore, provides a useful medium of communication for a group that wonders about the degree of trust and acceptance between the members, and puts the operation on a "professional" basis that does not require deep levels of personal trust or high levels of professional competence. It is thus a good method for making experimental moves into new situations and establishing new relationships.

I do not believe the case method will solve all the problems of parish pastors. But I do believe it is a method by which they can design their parish practice for professional self-development.

IX. Learning to Fight Like Christians in the Church

In these days of increasing conflict and controversy in the church, every pastor must develop professional skills for dealing with conflict creatively. This is a question to which I have devoted some thought, and a development that has attracted some of my preacher-watching. What follows is a sermon I have prepared for delivery in local congregations. As a traveling preacher who has the opportunity to preach the same sermon to many different congregations I have shared these thoughts with congregations North and South, large and small, urban and rural, black and white, and with groups in classrooms and conferences. As part of the Currie Lectures at Austin Seminary I presented this material in pretty much its present form, asking the ministers assembled for the lectures to evaluate it both as an analysis of the issue and as a homiletical event. Their response, and the response of the congregations who have heard it, encourage me to set it down here in that form. The texts are Jeremiah 8:8-11, Matthew 10:34-39, and I Corinthians 11:17-19.

A. PREACHING ON CONFLICT: A SERMON

"Can we learn to fight like Christians in the church?" That question is the subject of the sermon. And it is an attempt to get at a condition that seems more and more to characterize our contemporary life. There is an increasing amount of conflict, controversy, and polarization in the church and society. I do not think this is a "problem," as if there were a "solution." Nor do I see it as a "question" that is to be "answered." Life does not really consist of questions and answers, problems and solutions. Rather it is a condition in which we must learn to live as creatively and constructively as we can. There is a deep yearning across the church for something that will bring us together. But something deeper is needed.

As Christians, we are called to a ministry of reconciliation. This ministry is not simply to ourselves, as if "peace in the church" was an end in itself. On the contrary, we must learn to fight like Christians in the church because we are called to fight like Christians in the *world*. The purpose of our learning this in church is to equip us for our ministry in the world. How can an unreconciled church minister to an unreconciled world? It is not that we must settle all our differences in the church before we can venture forth in a ministry of reconciliation. But we must be toughened more for battle than most of us are today. We have learned how to avoid conflict and controversy. We must now learn to engage in it, not simply for ourselves, but for the deepening of our discipleship and the strengthening of our ministry. But how? Our question falls naturally into three parts: (1) what does it mean to *fight* (2) *in church* (3) *like Christians?*

1. What Is the Fight About?

When I suggest that we learn to *fight,* I certainly do not mean fisticuffs. We are not called to train in boxing, wrestling, karate, judo, or any other physical disciplines. I refer to the wrestling and contending that goes on among us in church, and has from the beginning. Paul writes to the Corinthians: "I hear there are divisions among you, and I partly believe it, for there must be factions among you so that those who are genuine may be recognized" (I Cor. 11:18-19). Paul was not surprised to find divisions and factions, conflict and controversy. He was concerned that their coming together as a church was "not for the better but for the worse" (11:17). What are the sources of this divisiveness in the church? There are at least four things that occur to me.

(a) It is a function of the way we are created as human beings. According to the ancient Scriptures, we are made "in the image of God." Whatever else this means, it teaches us that we are not made in the image of one another: no two human beings are exactly alike. We never do see things the same way, or feel the same way about them, or understand them exactly alike. This difference between us as human beings produces a certain amount of friction and tension. A line in *Music Man* says that people in Iowa can "stand nose to nose for days and days and never see eye to eye." We are sometimes advised to identify with others, to sit where they sit, to walk a mile in their shoes, etc. But that is a physical impossibility. If I am to sit where you sit, you must get up and move. Then you are no longer where you were! And if I am walking in your shoes, what are you wearing? So long as we are unique, human beings made in the image of God, and not identical carbon copies, there will be tension, friction, difficulty in understanding—conflict.

(b) Another factor that leads to friction results from some new developments in modern society. The "population explosion" means there are more people around, and so we run into more people, many of whom are different from those we are accustomed to meeting. "Population mobility" describes America, at least, as a people on the move. This brings us into contact with more and more people as they come and go. The increase in conflict among us, then, is not necessarily the result of a loss of national character or a decline in public morality. It is the result of the increased strain of adjusting to more people who differ more widely. So long as we travel widely, move from job to job, go off to college and military service, there will be more and more conflict. "Women's Lib" and the "generation gap" describe other developments that increase conflict and confrontation. A management magazine recently featured an article on "How to Handle Protesters at Your Annual Meeting." That is a problem that did not come up in the past! In the church the "clergy-laity" gap provides another source of conflict. In these and other ways, developments in modern society increase the amount of tension, conflict and controversy. None of them are evil, but they precipitate changes in established relationships. They "disturb the peace."

(c) If contemporary changes are not enough, ancient divisions persist among us. Deep suspicions and hostilities between nations, races, and creeds nurtured over generations will not go away. In my own experience I have become aware of the way in which I came to my sense of identity. As a WASP it was a negative sense of identity. I never really knew who I was, I just knew who I wasn't! I knew I was one of *us,* not one of *them.* It came to me like this.

I knew I was a Christian because I wasn't a Jew. I knew I was a Protestant because I wasn't a Catholic; a Presbyterian because I wasn't a Baptist, a Methodist, or an Episcopalian. I knew I was an American because I wasn't a foreigner. And I knew there was something special about me because I wasn't "colored." We told stories about all of *them*, to learn who *we* were. I could call this little exercise in self-analysis the confessions of a repentant white racist. But it is not as simple as that. Beginning with the fact that all of us are different from the rest of us, each group builds its sense of identity on their sense of difference from others. The significant difference, I now see, is that we WASPs achieved our sense of identity and integrity at the price of everyone else's. *We* were doing fine as long as *they* continued to act out our stereotypes. But when you met a Jew who didn't "look like a Jew," you were never quite sure again. When Catholics (especially since Vatican II) didn't "act like Catholics," we were not so sure what a Protestant was. And the first time you met a Baptist who drank and an Episcopalian who didn't, that stereotype was broken. When blacks quit shuffling for the amusement of "whitey" and black became beautiful, the meaning of "white" was not so clear. So ancient fears and hatreds, buried deep and sometimes smoothed over, erupt to disturb the status quo and unsettle the tranquillity of the body politic. As the prophet Jeremiah put it: "They have healed the wound of my people lightly, saying 'Peace, peace,' when there is no peace" (8:11). The wound is deep; it burst open. And even where it has healed there is a scar, reminding us of ancient hostilities that are gone but not forgotten. They must be dealt with, and that means learning a new way of relating.

(d) A fourth factor is the gospel itself. There is a text in Matthew's gospel which I have never liked. But everytime I open my Bible to chapter 10, verses 34-36, it is still there. It won't go away. It says: "Do not think that I have come to bring peace on earth; I have not come to bring peace, but a sword . . . to set a man against his father, and a daughter against her mother

. . . and a man's foes will be those of his own house-
hold."

Nobody in his right mind preaches the gospel just to
cause trouble. But one of the things we know about the
gospel is that it calls into question every human relationship and commitment. As Matthew's text puts it,
at verse 37, "He who loves father or mother more than
me is not worthy of me." The preaching of the gospel
can produce conflict, controversy, and division—even
in a family—since the call is to "follow me." Thus the
Christian religion, itself, contributes to the conflict in
society and in the church. So it is not enough to say:
let's all get religion. Religion, itself, may be the cause
of some of the controversy.

There is another element, an important one. Since
the gospel is for all (II Cor. 5:14-15), the church, as the
bearer of the gospel, has bought into every issue that
divides men from one another. The gospel is not just
for old or young—so we straddle the generation gap.
It is not just for black or white—so we are caught in
racial tensions. It is not for Americans only—so we
are into international relations. It is not only for men
or women—so we must reckon with women's lib and
male chauvinism. If we are called to a ministry of reconciliation (II Cor. 5:17-20) then we are called to minister in all places where men and women and children
are separated, divided, hostile, alienated, in conflict.
This is why we must learn to fight like Christians in
the church! Not so we can get along with one another,
but so we will be strengthened for the mission and ministry to which we are called. That is what the *fight* is
about. At least some of it. But what does it mean to
fight *in church?* More important, how can we *learn*
to fight in church?

2. Why Fight in Church?

This seems, at first, a shocking suggestion. But let me put you at ease at two points. First, we have always done a lot of fighting in church. I grew up in the church, and one of the first things I learned was that people in church will fight about almost anything: the color of the rug, the personal habits of the preacher, the kind of literature used in the church school—the list seems endless. I do not worry about *starting* a fight in a church, but I do worry about how that fighting can become more constructive. The *Good News For Modern Man* translation renders I Cor. 11:17 like this: "Your church meetings actually do more harm than good." Second, we have domesticated the idea of conflict in a number of interesting ways. Look at the hymnal in your church. There is probably a section entitled "Christian Warfare," and in the section on "The Christian Life" there will be some reference to conflict. I have checked a few. In the Evangelical and Reformed *Hymnal* "Conflict and Victory" is classified after "Love and Fellowship" and before "Comfort and Trust." The *Pilgrim Hymnal* lists "Pilgrimage and Conflict" between "Faith and Aspiration" and "Consecration." *The Methodist Hymnal* has a section entitled "Courage in Conflict" after "Hope, Joy, and Peace" and before "Prayer and Aspiration." In this very simple way "conflict" is catalogued as part of the "Christian life" and accepted as a category in the hymnal. A minor point, but interesting.

3. Violence in America

But more important than these ecclesiastical expressions are some secular signs that we have learned to fight *outside* the church. In learning to fight like Christians in the church, we can begin by building on what we have learned about fighting elsewhere. We have not seen ourselves as a violent people, but in America we have learned to tolerate quite a lot of conflict, controversy, and violence in at least three areas of our lives. There are clues we can follow in sports, law, and business.

"Sports": Conflict for Fun and Profit. If a visitor from another planet were to drop to earth on New Year's Day and find himself in front of a color television set watching football games back to back, he would probably not know what to make of this. Try to imagine what it would be like to see this for the first time: great hulking humans, dressed for combat, rushing, kicking, tackling, pulling, charging, smashing. And all this violence to get a little leather ball through some poles at the end of the field! If our interplanetary visitor were a sensitive being he would probably be shocked and cry out to stop the violence.

But we explain to him that this is what we call a "game". We point out first of all the esthetic quality of the activity: the beautiful green field with the pretty white lines and colorful flags, the colorful uniforms, and the happy crowd. Then we point out how well organized things are. The men do not just attack one another at random. They line up in neat formations, crash into one another, stop, line up again, and begin the process over again. And there are limits to what they can do. We point out the men in the striped shirts who every once in awhile throw down their pretty colored handkerchiefs and say "no-no." If we can convince our visitor that the violence is controlled and contained, that the combat will not spread to the spectators in the stands, that there are rules of the game, officials in charge, and score being kept, perhaps he can relax (as we do) and watch the violence without offense and, perhaps, even some enjoyment. We could argue from economics as well, pointing out how much the players earn by this activity, how much income it brings to the city, the taxes that support community services, etc.

The fact is that professional football is a violent activity. But when we call it a "game" and play according to the rules, we can tolerate this kind of conflict—and even enjoy it. Conflict for fun and profit.

Imagine now that we take our visitor on a tour of our town. We want to show him how we live, how cultured and civilized we are. So we take him to church with us. He sits with us in our pew as we participate in the service. He notes the dignified man in the black robe who presides, and the people who sit with him in the choir loft. The atmosphere is one of respect and reverence. Our visitor becomes a little nervous as the minister warms to his subject and raises his voice. But when he sees that no one objects, he relaxes. He is, of course, a little surprised when the people shake the minister's hand after the service and thank him for shouting at them. He does not know what all this means, but he sees that we understand, and we continue our tour of the town.

"Order in the Court": Conflict and Justice. We take him to a building that may look something like a church, a large imposing building near the center of the town. We walk up the steps and into a large chamber finished in wood paneling, with pews for the audience and furnishings in the front for a dignified man in a black robe. A dozen people sit together in what looks like a choir loft, with some chairs and tables arranged behind a kind of altar rail. A man rises and calls for order, a hush falls over the room, and the proceedings begin. The pace of action and the tone of voices are dignified, measured, almost reverent. An attractive lady of middle age is called to the front to take a seat near the man in the black robe, and another gentleman rises and approaches her. He most courteously asks her name and inquires about her personal activities.

She answers calmly and graciously. But suddenly the relationship changes. The man begins to press her with pry-
ing questions; he succeeds in embarrassing her and confusing her. The more she stumbles in her replies the more
relentlessly he presses his questions. Eventually the woman
begins to weep and looks to the kindly man in the black
robe for help. He is unmoved.

Our visitor from outer space turns to us and asks why
we do not stop this persecution of the nice lady. So we
explain to him that this is a court of law. The man behind the bench is the judge. The people sitting with him
up front are not the choir, but the jury. The lady is a
witness. The man questioning her is the prosecutor. And
we explain to him that—as strange as it may seem to him
—in our society we believe that out of this conflict of
prosecution and defense we reach the truth and achieve
justice, that out of the open conflict of opposing interests
and points of view we accomplish something constructive.
He will probably find this hard to believe, but we realize
that we have grown accustomed to this way of doing things,
and have developed quite a tolerance for active conflict
and controversy in another area of our lives.

Competition, Freedom, and Profit: The American Way.
Next we take our visitor for luncheon with us to our
civic club's weekly meeting. After the lunch we sit back
to listen to the speaker of the day. He represents a national
organization concerned to promote free enterprise and
economic freedom. As he warms to his subject he begins to
speak in glowing terms of the need for competition in
business to produce better products. He insists that govern-
ment supervision and controls lead to lethargy and poor
products. Competition in the open market, conflict between competing companies, is necessary to maintain our
way of life, to provide for all our people better products at
a lower price. Our visitor is confused again. "You really

believe that conflict between companies produces better products?" Yes, we say, we have come not only to accept conflict in the marketplace, but to embrace it as a good thing. He does not understand. But we do. In yet another area of our lives we have learned how to harness conflict for ends in which we believe.

We have learned to fight in court, in business, and on football fields. Can we learn to fight in church? It appears to me that, when we know the "name of the game" the "rules of the game" and learn to "play fair according to the rules" we can tolerate very high levels of conflict. Curiously enough it is often those who engage most actively in these worldly battles who are most opposed to "fighting in church." "We do that all week," they say. "When we come to church we want to get away from all that." I understand the feeling. But I am also convinced that these centurions who have learned to do battle in sports, law, and business can be some of our best teachers when it comes to learning to fight like Christians in the church.

What is needed, it seems to me, is a kind of "game" we can play which will provide the opportunity to put these learnings into practice. Those with little experience can begin by "playing the game." The pastor can provide the initial leadership, but first he must learn to play. So here is a game with which he can begin. It provides a way by which we can begin to learn to fight like Christians in the church.

4. Learning to Fight Like Christians

The first step is to design an activity that allows us, through conflict in the church, to achieve the values we profess. If, in sports, violence can be organized to produce entertainment, sportsmanship, and profit; the legal struggle in the court can produce justice; and competition in business can produce better products—how can we structure conflict in the church so it leads to faith, hope, and love, the kingdom of God, and an effective ministry of reconciliation in the gospel?

B. TRAINING IN CONFLICT: A GAME

I have developed a "conflict game" for use in local churches. The game is based on four principles: containment, clarity, consideration, and commitment. For each principle there are simple rules. No group can play this game unless they can agree on ground rules and trust someone to guide them through the game under the rules. This indicates the responsibility of the pastor in structuring and directing the activity.

1. Containment

One thing that keeps people from entering into conflict situations is the fear that the conflict will get out of hand, out of control. It is important, therefore, for the pastor to take responsibility for designing ground rules and limits for the game. It may also be important for him to be, or not to be, the referee.

(a) Time limits. When the group is new at the game, the time limit can be very brief. Try thirty minutes to begin. The first rule is simple: at the end of thirty minutes the game is over. Anyone should be able to sit through thirty minutes of conflict, but everyone will be happier if the end is in sight.

(b) Space limits. The group agrees to stay within a given physical boundary, like a room or within fifteen feet of a tree. The point is to keep the group together, but to allow people freedom to look away, move around, or to sit still—whatever the ground rules are.

(c) Size of the group. Only those who agree to play are allowed in the game. There is no provision for observers or spectators, unless the group decides to allow them. The point is to play the game. Those who don't believe they are ready to play can be allowed to watch. If, after watching others play, they want into the game, they can join at a time specified.

(d) The leader. Someone must be chosen as "referee." Someone must be in charge, to call the "plays," to declare what is "out of bounds," to protect the group against those who will not play by the rules.

Just as a prize fight is legal when there is a ring (space limits), rounds (time limits), and a referee, so a group of Christians can have a legal fight when they have the ground rules and the personnel.

2. Clarity

Rule: no one has the right to agree or disagree with another person's position until he has been able to state the other person's position to his satisfaction.

I discovered that a lot of conflict comes from misunderstanding as well as from disagreement. In meetings people would agree with what I said and then vote against me. I decided they had not understood. And, in my declining years, I have come to the conclusion that I would rather be disagreed with by someone who understands me, than to be agreed with by someone who does not understand me. Understanding, not agreement, is the name of the game. This takes time. But if the group is not willing to take time to understand, there is no point in playing.

3. Consideration

Rule: no one has a right to speak twice until everyone who wants to speak has had a change to speak once.

This is a defense against people like me and all the

fast jaws and quick tongues in the crowd. The group must defend itself against the glib and take time to hear those who are not so quick of tongue. There are some ways to play the game that help.

One is to use a "timekeeper." If you have ten people and are going to fight for thirty minutes, that means everyone has only three minutes.

Another device is "rounds." Each player has a piece of paper with a mark on one side. The other side is blank. When a player speaks he turns his card over. In this way the chairman can see who has spoken and who hasn't. When almost everyone has spoken the chairman says: "A lot of us have spoken. Is there anyone who wants to speak in this round before we open the second round?" If anybody asks to be heard, the group waits for him before going into the second round. If nobody wants to speak, then the cards are turned over and the second round begins.

Another device is "tickets." If you have ten people and have decided to fight for thirty minutes, this means everyone has three minutes. Each person then gets three tickets, worth one minute each. I have seen this played out in different ways. Some people want to make a speech right at the start, use up their three minutes, and sit silently (if uneasily) through the rest of the game. Others sneak in a comment here and there, using up their tickets one at a time. Still others wait until the end and use all their tickets to have the last word. And in some groups, I have even seen people give their tickets away, to let someone else have more time!

4. Commitment

Rule: the only way to "score" is to use things that "count." This is a decision the group must make in advance. My suggestion for a "scoring system" is based on the Protestant tradition in which I stand. In this system there are only three things that count for Christians in the church: the Bible, the historic faith, and one's own personal commitment to Jesus Christ as Lord.

If these are used as "counters," then nothing else counts. Not statistics, or what's good for business, or what people say, or what your grandma taught you—nothing but Scripture, tradition, and commitment. This is at least a way to begin, but each group must decide what it will mean for them to "fight like Christians in the church."

I've seen this work in churches in the South in arguments over "the race question." I consider myself a kind of liberal, and I can't say that some of my best friends are segregationists. But I do know that when we fight—and stick to the rules—I learn something I didn't know before. I hear texts quoted from the Bible I had never heard before. And I have had people tell me that they thought it was their Christian duty to work to keep the races separate. I didn't agree with them. But I came to understand that, for them, this was the best way they knew to be faithful to Jesus Christ as Lord. And I had to score my points in the same way—quoting the Bible, taking my stand in the Christian faith, and finally making my own testimony on the basis of my Christian commitment. Sometime we feel like we have "won" or "lost," but more often than not we have the feeling that everyone has gained a little. That feeling is expressed in a "games theory" that describes two kinds of games.

I used to think that in every game somebody won and somebody lost, and that the only difference was that some games were played for "fun" and others were played for "keeps." Now I have learned that, whether for fun or keeps, there is another distinction between kinds of games. *Zero-sum games* have a fixed "pot." No matter how the game is played, the players cannot win any more than is in the pot. Somebody wins and somebody loses. *Non-zero-sum games* do not have a fixed "pot." The size of the pot depends on how the game is played. If the group plays well, there is more in the pot at the end of the game, so "everybody wins." But if the group plays poorly, there may be less—or nothing at all—when the game is over, so "everybody loses." This is an important distinction.

My experience has been that, when Christians play this conflict game, everybody wins. Understanding is deepened, consideration is learned, and the limits of people for conflict are tested and stretched. I realize that this is a parlor game. It just won't work when people are at one another's throats crying for blood. But there's a lot of work to be done this side of the battlefront, in a kind of de-militarized zone.

Telling people they shouldn't fight won't do any good. Nor will it do to insist that everyone must get into every conflict in the congregation. People have very different levels of tolerance for conflict and controversy. No one can be made to fight against his will. At the same time, those who want to contend for what they believe in should not be kept from conflict if they are willing to fight by the rules. Can we learn to fight like Christians in the church? I believe we can. I know we must. I hope this game will help.

X. Specialized/ Experimental Parish Ministries

By now we have our passive pastor moving along. He has made some personal moves to overcome his passivity and break out of the conform/complaint syndrome. He has mastered some professional methods that break the bitch/ brag syndrome. He is paying his rent, developing his career. He has joined the Academy of Parish Clergy and is working with his colleagues to develop professional skills for dealing with parish problems. He is running risks, handling conflict, and driving demons from his date-book. He is a creative and effective pastor. He has discovered his professional specialty and is becoming more competent in the practice of parish ministry. He knows the parish ministry is not a seamless garment that he must take as a whole or leave alone. He perceives its component parts and is learning to vary them one at a time on an experimental basis. What other options does he have?

In this next section I want to present very briefly the outlines of some specialized ministries that require a parish as their base. It is often assumed that a pastor must leave the parish to be specialized and experimental. These models suggest options for the pastor who has paid his parish rent and wants to experiment.

A. MINISTRY OF DIAGNOSIS AND REFERRAL: EXPERIMENTING WITH THE PASTORAL ROLE

An increasing number of people in our society have difficulties and do not know what to do about them.

When they get desperate enough, they will go to the most immediately visible, available, and accessible professional and ask for help. People seldom get to the proper professional on the first try. This is partly because, in an increasingly mobile society, people just don't know what their problems are or who can help them. At the same time, certain professionals are becoming increasingly invisible and inaccessible. More and more doctors have their offices in high-rise buildings near hospitals. Lawyers cluster around court houses. This provides the possibility for a specialized and experimental parish-based ministry of diagnosis and referral.

The parish clergy are the most generally deployed professionals in the community, scattered fairly evenly across the landscape. They are also readily accessible by telephone, often have time on their schedule to see people, and have offices in buildings with convenient parking nearby. They can often be seen in emergencies without advance appointments, and seldom charge fees for services. The pastor who wants to "re-invest" some of his professional expertise in the counseling role after having "paid his rent" can develop a significant specialized experimental ministry of diagnosis and referral. Whether or not there is any theological justification for it, there is a need in our society for this service. Pastors can provide it.

A study made in the early 1960s by the National Institutes of Mental Health reported that 42 percent of all persons seeking assistance with marital problems turned first to a clergyman! They turned to other professionals in the following percentages:

General practitioners in medicine   25 percent
Marriage counselors or family service   18 percent
Psychiatrists and psychologists   12 percent

In 1964, the NIMH granted funds for a special program to train seminary professors in pastoral care on the grounds that by doing this they could increase the professional competence of clergymen as counselors and thereby make a substantial contribution to preventive mental health. There is a demonstrated need for service. Pastors can meet this need. What model of ministry is required?

A parish minister, after paying his parish rent, may experiment with a specialized ministry of diagnosis and referral. He makes himself available to troubled people as a point of entry into the professional resources of the community. He develops skill in helping people understand the nature of their difficulties (diagnosis), and he also becomes knowledgeable about the professional resources of the community (referral). He may also develop a "professional specialty" of his own so that, in principle, he may refer some people to himself as the most qualified and available professional resource in the community.

There is a present need for this ministry, and the need will grow in the future. As population mobility accelerates, people have increasing difficulty in establishing relationships in new communities with professionals they can trust and afford. The roles of professionals are changing, and it is difficult for the average person to know what kind of professional assistance he needs. Here is a job description for a pastor who wants to do a piece of the world's work and do it as a specialized and experimental parish ministry.

B. THE PARISH PASTOR AS A CATALYST IN THE INDEPENDENT SECTOR

As pastor of a parish, the minister has an identification in the local community as a professional at work in the independent sector. As leader of a voluntary organization committed to good works, he is often called upon to serve on the Boy Scout Council, the Human Relations Commission, the Mayor's Youth Advisory Council, etc. The parish pastor who wants to experiment with this style of ministry does not have to leave his parish to do so. He simply has to develop ways to experiment in his parish that free him for this kind of ministry. A specific model is suggested by Donald Shriver. He has spent many years in a campus ministry. In that role he experienced the marginality of a minister with a vague job description. But instead of complaining about it as a problem, he conceived some possibilities in it. One is the idea of "the functional uses of marginality." Here are two ways it might work out.

When the role of a particular professional is not clear to other people, he can usually get in to see them. Shriver suggests that a pastor can get an appointment with almost anyone in town. If you want an appointment with the mayor, he is likely to give you one—precisely because he cannot figure out in advance how to handle you. He has to see you to find out! Your marginality gives you an appointment. It may not give you any influence, but it gives you an opening.

Another thing a pastor can do is call meetings. This may not seem to be a very important thing, but in certain instances it is the decisive action required to aid the community in dealing with its problems. During the days of strictest segregation in the South, authorities were hesitant to break up a church meeting, even if it was integrated. The pastor is one of the few professionals in the community who has both the power to call a meeting and a place to hold it! A pastor who does not use his power of invitation is overlooking an important aspect of his professionality. In a changing society when roles are changing, the minister can take initiative in all sorts of matters. This is precisely *because* of his marginality. While many ministers cry for the clarification of their image, more ministers ought to consider the functional uses of their marginality.

In response to a lot of talk about "the church in the world" some pastors have concluded that they must leave the parish in order to encounter the world. This is silly. Locality is always one ingredient in the parish. In this sense the world is always in the church. The pastor who wants to design an experimental ministry can experiment with the community as a variable. And one point at which he can begin is with his fellow professionals in the community. What we need now is "occupational ecumenism," assembling the professional cadre of a community for relevant and effective action. Although the pastor has no "authority" to do this, he is a natural one to seize the initiative. If he is concerned about the whole person, he knows he cannot meet all the needs of any person. The professional resources of the community tend not to be well deployed. Some professionals overlap and compete, while whole areas of the community go untended. As a catalyst in the community, the pastor can assemble those professionals who are willing to look at the total community, not just in terms of their special interests and concerns, but as a whole.

Another aspect of occupational ecumenism is the need for the pastor to be part of a network of professional resources in the community. It is not enough for him to get the ministers together across denominational lines, he must work to bring practitioners together across professional lines. As a community catalyst he can use his marginality, his skills as a convener and presider, to develop an experimental parish-based ministry.

C. SOCIAL CHANGE IN THE PARISH

The pastor can work at the issue of "social change" in the parish by using the congregation experimentally. I hear the argument that the church resists change, as if other social institutions are not resistant to change. I believe that the church is really no more resistant to change than most other social organizations with which I am familiar. Anyone who has tried to change the curriculum in a theological seminary, or the recipe for spaghetti at the P.T.A. supper knows this is true. One of the problems pastors have in effecting change in the parish is the assumption that a majority must always approve before changes can be made. While it is true that voluntary organizations require a rather high degree of consensus in order to function, and provision needs to be made to protect the minority against the majority, pastors also need to get smart about the fact that significant minorities can change institutions.

I work on the theory that from 10 to 20 percent of the congregation are essentially liberal, forward-looking and open to change. At the other extreme, from 10 to 20 percent of the membership will be conservative, closed-minded, and resistant to change. This leaves anywhere from 60 to 80 percent of the constituency in the middle, a kind of "silent majority." One thing I have learned about silent majorities is that they prefer their majority status to their silence. Another is that they are passive practitioners of the conform/complaint syndrome. This means that they are ready to identify with whatever appears to be the majority. Therefore the pastor need only worry about "tipping the balance." If he can get from 5 to 10 percent of the middle group to identify with either a change-assisting or a change-resisting strategy, he can determine the direction of the movement in the parish.

By using just one of the congregational variables on a kind of "sliding scale" the pastor can experiment with various strategies of social change. The congregation, itself, becomes an instrument of social change in the community mix. Through marshaling the congregation the pastor can effect social change in the community much more directly and permanently. The pastor who flees his congregation to be "socially relevant" is overlooking one of the major components in a change strategy for the community. Once again, the pastor does not have to leave the parish to get into the "world." His parish is part of the world, and provides the setting for a specialized and experimental ministry.

D. MEASURING MINISTERIAL EFFECTIVENESS

When the pastor seeks to be creative, exploring new specialized and experimental ministries in the parish, it will be more difficult to measure his effectiveness. He will need to state his objectives much more clearly when he steps outside conventional roles and traditional patterns. What follows is an attempt to describe a place to start.

Much of the language about effectiveness in ministry reveals the bitch/brag syndrome. While many pastors pretend to have little concern about evaluating their performance, most ministers I know would like to do better at it. It will be easiest to start at those points at which the question comes up most naturally, as in the five following situations.

(a) When the pastor *feels* ineffective. He asks himself: "What am I really accomplishing by all the work I am doing? What difference does it make?" This sounds like the conform/complaint syndrome—but it is less a complaint than a call for clarity and thus a form of the bitch/brag syndrome.

(b) When the pastor *fears* effectiveness. He fears that he will "manipulate" people, that he will be overbearing, authoritarian. This fear reflects his perception that he has some real power, that he is potentially effective, and it scares him. He cannot use his power freely and effectively until he breaks out of the syndrome.

(c) When the pastor wants to *focus* his effectiveness. He intends one effect, but something else happens. Like a marksman, he wants to improve his aim. When he preaches on brotherhood and the level of racism in his parish goes up or he plans a stewardship program and the contributions go down, he will be concerned about the focus of his effectiveness, not simply the force of it or his feelings about it.

(d) When the pastor faces competition. When a pastor begins to compare his performance with that of his colleagues, the question comes up: "Am I as effective as the other fellow?"

In each instance the pastor is tempted to fall into the bitch/brag syndrome, to express his feelings of under-effectiveness or his fear of over-effectiveness. The temptation is to flee to some island of ambiguity where he can escape the necessity of facing the realities of his situation.

There are also some points in the ministerial career when the question comes up with special force and clarity.

(a) Entry into the profession. One of the concerns of young people considering any career is for effectiveness: "What difference will it make?" This is a natural concern, and it must be reckoned with. Especially in any efforts at recruiting, we must be sure to present an accurate and honest picture of the profession. There are some things a minister can do, and other things he cannot do. Every profession has its possibilities and its limitations. Serious concerns about both personal and professional effectiveness come to focus at the point of entry.

(b) Turning points in the career. Every time a pastor moves from one parish to another it is natural for him to assess his past effectiveness and to estimate his future effectiveness. With the passage of time, a pastor has an opportunity to observe himself in a variety of roles and settings. A minister who functions well in one setting might not do so well in another. Reflection on this factor helps the pastor estimate his effectiveness in terms of situational specializations. A minister who performs well in one role will not necessarily perform well in the others. Estimation of his effectiveness in various roles helps him measure his effectiveness in terms of skill specializations. (For a fuller discussion of these factors see *Profession: Minister*, pp. 117 ff.)

There are personal turning points as well as professional ones. Personal interests, family responsibilities, and physical stamina change along with professional capabilities. The pastor must take these into account in measuring his effectiveness.

(c) Ending the career. At the end of the professional career it is appropriate to look back and ask: "What effect has my ministry had? What difference did I make?" At this point the pastor is not concerned to evaluate his effectiveness as a basis for further professional development, but to achieve some sense of personal integrity. It is a natural concern, a question the pastor must try to answer.

At every point the bitch/brag syndrome is complicated by the persistence of pastoralia. We have already demythologized one of the most popular ("You know, a minister never knows how much *good* he is doing") by putting it into the demythologizer, and pushing the "reverse" button. It comes out: "You know, a minister never knows how much *harm* he is doing." The pastor is going to have an effect—one way or the other. How can that effect be described and measured?

I use a simple device, similar in some respects to the change-grid. It is based on the assumption that the primary task of the pastor is not to define effectiveness but to describe the effects of his ministry. "Effectiveness" is an abstraction. "Effects" are concrete, describable, and therefore measurable. How can they be identified and described? I ask three simple questions:

1. What are the effects of your ministry?
What do you do that has any effect?
2. What skills do you have that produce these effects?
How did you learn to do these things?
3. What do you think would make your ministry more effective? What kinds of things would you need to know and be able to do to increase your effectiveness?

In using this device I have discovered that many ministers are really pretty sharp about what they are doing. They need only to be asked specific questions about what they know, and be given some assurance that what they are doing is worth reporting.

Once these identifications have been made, it is helpful to try to put the data into the form of a chart. Here is a whimsical "Parish Rector Rating Chart" prepared by Robert Rodenmayer. It shows how we can identify "performance measures" and describe "performance degrees" for measuring effectiveness. What is needed now is some systematic data-gathering to identify the aspects of pastoral performance that must be measured, and to articulate the various levels of performance. Without this, pastors are left only with bodies, bucks, and bricks (members, budget, and buildings) by which to measure their performance. We must find those things that "count," not only the things that are easy to measure. This is a task that all

PARISH RECTOR RATING CHART

	PERFORMANCE DEGREES	
PERFORMANCE MEASURES	Far Exceeds Requirements	Exceeds Requirements
ADAPTABILITY	Leaps tall obstacles with a single bound	Must take a running start to leap over tall obstacles
PASTORAL CALLING	Is faster than a speeding bullet	Is as fast as a speeding bullet
STRENGTH OF CHARACTER	Is stronger than a herd of bulls	Is stronger than several bulls
SPIRITUAL MATURITY	Walks on water consistently	Walks on water in emergencies
PREACHING	Enthralls huge throngs	Enthralls his congregation
COMMUNICATION	Talks with God	Talks with the angels

Meets Requirements	Needs Some Improvement	Does Not Meet Minimum Requirements
Can leap over small obstacles only	Crashes into obstacles when attempting to jump over them	Cannot recognize obstacles at all
Not quite as fast as a speeding bullet	Would you believe a slow bullet	Usually wounds self with bullet
Is stronger than one bull	Shoots the bull	Smells like a bull
Swims in water	Washes in water	Drinks water
Interests his congregation	Only his wife listens to him	Not even his wife listens to him
Talks with himself	Argues with himself	Loses arguments with himself

Courtesy R. N. Rodenmayer 1968

pastors must undertake, hopefully through the Academy of Parish Clergy. The work has already begun. Here is the preliminary attempt of a task force of the Academy to identify the "competences" required for parish ministry.

E. COMPETENCE IN THE MINISTRY

In order to function effectively under the pressures of parish practice, pastors must possess an operational understanding of their ministry. This operational understanding of parish ministry is also essential for those who plan for theological education both in preparation for ministry and in post-ordination training.

To do his work in the parish a pastor must develop basic skills in each of the five areas demanding his professional competence: (1) responding to his particular situation, (2) managing his parish organization, (3) relating to individuals, (4) developing his own personal and professional resources and (5) planning and providing for public worship.

1. Competence in relating effectively to congregations in their particular social, economic, political, and cultural context demands situational skills that do not necessarily transfer from one context to another:
   a. skills in communicating, e.g. preaching and writing.
   b. skills in interpreting the religious heritages to contemporary life.
   c. skills in interpreting life issues in terms of both inherited and emerging religious symbols.
   d. skills in understanding and providing for the social, recreational, and amusement life of the church.
   e. skills in helping the congregation to effect change in its community.
2. Competence in the management of religious organizations requires the following skills:
   a. skills in effective participation in and leadership of groups.

    b. skills in assistance to a religious organization in identifying and achieving its goals.

    c. skills in recruitment of persons for the organization and for jobs within the organization.

    d. skills in management functions, e.g. planning, organizing, directing and evaluating.

    e. skills in supervision within the voluntary organization.

    f. sociological and political analysis of the congregation and the communities to which it is related.

    g. skills in creative handling of conflict.

    h. skills in money and property management.

3. Competence in helping individuals to acquire maturity, health, and strength requires these skills:

    a. skills in teaching.

    b. skills in leading people in their personal spiritual lives.

    c. skills in counseling and referrals.

    d. skills in responding effectively to people's expectations of his role.

4. Competence in developing his own personal and professional resources involves the following skills:

    a. skills in using the case study method, e.g., action-reflection.

    b. skills in developing the inner-life, e.g., prayer and meditation.

    c. skills in confronting his own beliefs, convictions, and doubts in the light of heritage.

    d. skills in identifying a need for professional assistance and making use of consultative services.

    e. skills in making use of opportunities for career development and continuing education.

    f. skills in dealing with his own expectations of himself.

5. Competence in developing and leading public worship necessitates the use of nearly all the skills identified in the other four areas.[1]

---

[1] From *The Journal of The Academy of Parish Clergy*, April, 1971, pp. 63-64.

The text of this "working draft" is included here, not to reveal a finished product, but to recruit pastors for an ongoing task. Reactions and suggestions should be sent to the Academy of Parish Clergy, 3100 West Lake Street, Minneapolis, Minnesota 55416.

One of the by-products of the case method is a concern for stating objectives and measuring effectiveness. (See Chapter VIII.) I encourage pastors to address these matters in specific, concrete, terms. If they want to build up some general objectives or some general norms for effectiveness, that is their business. As for me, I prefer to press two simple questions: (1) What were your objectives in this event, and (2) what effects did your ministry have in this event? If enough of these questions are answered in relation to enough specific cases, the individual pastor will develop a base of data from which to identify his general objectives in ministry and formulate the norms by which he can evaluate his effectiveness.

The transition from specific findings to general statements is not as difficult as the reverse. If the pastor can see himself in the process of setting objectives and assessing his effectiveness, he has a basis on which to identify the general objectives and norms he is actually using. Then he can decide whether these meet his formal standards or not. But if he starts with his formal notions, he is not likely ever to get to the point where he can use them for any practical purpose.

Nothing has more potential for theological education than the efforts of pastors to identify and measure effectiveness in ministry. It is not enough simply to demythologize existing pastoralia and break out of the bitch/brag syndrome. Constructive and creative efforts are required. In our seminary, at least, we are determined to design our professional education to meet the needs of the changing profession. But without the active and sustained support of practicing ministers we are left only to our own devices. Let this be an invitation to all who read this book to contribute to the process.

XI. A New Kind of Partnership

This book is not written to state conclusions, as if questions have been answered and problems have been solved. It is my part of a continuing conversation with clergymen about the parish ministry of the church. So here at the end I want to indicate the kinds of "loose ends" that still hang out, the directions in which I want to work. In *Profession: Minister* I referred briefly to the case method, conflict, and career development. I was still working on those things and had nothing to report. In this book I have dealt with those matters at some length, and have referred to some other issues that now concern me but about which I do not have much to say. They are management skills for the parish pastor, planning as a process for the renewal of the local church, and the development of a new kind of practical theology which will develop in dialogue between the seminary and parish pastors. On these final pages I want to sketch some proposals for the development of this parish-based and pastor-produced practical theology, and for the redirection of theological education toward more effective professional education for ministry.

A. PRACTICAL THEOLOGY IN THE PARISH

For too long pastors have believed that theologizing was the task of the seminaries, and that all they could do was translate and "apply" what the schools had taught them. Right now we need a new kind of dialogue between seminary and parish in which a genuine two-way conversation is possible. There is still much that seminaries can teach, but there is much we in the seminaries need to learn about the practice of ministry today. We can only learn this if pastors break out of the conform/complaint syndrome and start talking back to us. And that requires overcoming the bitch/brag syndrome too. What we need is the truth about the nature of the ministry today, told in clear and sensible terms.

As a suggested point of departure, I want to gather up some of the things I have put together that might point to a new discipline of practical theology, a discipline based in the parish, not in the seminary. It is intellectual, but not academic. Its purpose is not publication, but research and development. What is needed now is a network of pastors, working together with social scientists, theologians, and other professionals.

The primary contribution of pastors will be data-gathering. Through the use of the case method, change-grid, and other rudimentary research devices we can move toward the development of large-scale research projects of consequence. Some progress has been made with "information systems" that report parish innovations. The Innovation Referral Service of the United Methodist Board of Education is one example. There are others. The APC is developing communication networks between pastors working on similar projects. The late and lamented Ministry Studies Board tried one approach, failed to carry it off, but left some learning from which we can profit.

All these data cry out for theological reflection. Unless and until these data become the basis for pastoral theology and theological education, we continue to prepare today's ministers for yesterday's church, biblically literate, ethically sensitive, theologically articulate, and professionally incompetent. Pastors must assume responsibility for part of the theological task and make a contribution to the total enterprise.

A Note on Theological Method

In traditional theology, each field develops in relationship to a coordinate "secular" discipline on which it depends for methodology. Thus linguistics becomes the handmaiden of scripture study, historical scholarship supports church history, and philosophy assists systematic theology. We have become so used to these disciplines around the seminary that they have become accepted by many as "theological disciplines." Some biblical scholars, parsing verbs, think they are "doing theology." They are not. They are doing linguistics. They are ordering the data for theological reflection. This is important work, but is it theology?

Practical Theology has need of similar "secular" disciplines—to aid in the ordering of data for theological reflection. Some systematic theologians are finding studies of perception by psychologists helpful in the hermeneutical task; historians are discovering sociology. It has become acceptable to do theology linguistically, historically, and philosophically. It is now time to learn how to do theology sociologically, psychologically, anthropologically. No less rigor is required, but the disciplines must be developed by those who choose to do theology with the life and work of the church as data. This is the difference, for me, between Practical Theology and the other disciplines. The traditional disciplines deal with documents, records, artifacts. Practical Theology deals with the changing life of the church in the world. These data are much harder to order. The behavioral sciences are required to order the data for reflection, lest what appears to be "theological" is only bad sociology. This was the point of the chapter on "The Status of the Ministerial Profession" in *Profession: Minister*. Theologians and churchmen had been bemoaning the declining status of the clergyman. I set out to see if, on the basis of sociological studies of occupations, this was a fact. It proved not to be a fact at all. I decided right then and there that the next steps in Practical Theology required the development of disciplines to get at the truth about the life of the church in the world today. For too long we have taken antique sociological notions and tried to "apply" them to the contemporary church. "Koinonia groups" appear to succeed primarily where the social-psychological dynamics of group life are honored, not simply where correct theology is taught. The new turn toward "action-reflection" theology grows out of a felt need on the part of action-oriented Christians for a new method of theologizing that can begin with what they are actually doing in their life and work as Christians. It is a sad state of affairs when intelligent pastors are afraid to assume intellectual leadership in the life of the church, largely because they do not think they have a right to do it. I have tried all sorts of ways to help pastors develop their ability to theologize—mostly by assuring them that it is all right for them to do so.

The new discipline of practical theology will begin with a serious study of the life and work of the church. What the pastor does is grist for the theological mill—not just what the theologian says. How this truth, become flesh and dwelling among us, can become data for theological reflection is what we work at in the case method. It is hard to train pastors to think theologically about their work. They have been taught to think theology is only for the professor. And yet this is what the prophets of old did. They looked at their life and times, the affairs of kings and priests, life in the temple and in the marketplace, and they sought *in the events of their time* the Word of God. This is what I want for pastors, and nothing more: a disciplined attempt to seek in the events of their daily work the Word of God. If God is not at work in the work of ministry, where are we to seek? If we cannot see in the events of our life before God the meaning of these events, where shall we look?

I know, I know. God is at work outside the church. I believe that. But I also believe he is at work inside the church. The pastor, therefore, in reflecting on his daily task has a place to begin with his theologizing. He has access to data that are available to no one else. I do not advocate a new kind of gnosticism in which the pastor hides behind a haze of private perceptions. Far from it. The pastor must be able to make the shape of his work clear to others, as well as to himself. He must be able to make public, for all to see, the shape of the life he lives and the work he does. Then, with his colleagues, he seeks the meaning of that life and work as one clue to the meaning of the life of man before God. It is not the best piece, or even the most important one. But it is an essential piece—without which the total picture cannot be drawn.

B. PROFESSIONAL EDUCATION IN THE SEMINARY

But what are the professors in the seminary to be doing while the pastors in the parish are developing their theology? What is required, I am convinced, is a new sense of accountability on the part of the seminary to the ministry as a profession, the seminary as a professional school, and students as emerging professionals. Accountability to the profession is primary. The seminary is the servant of the church and its ministry. Although it must "pay rent" to the academic world to keep its accreditation, academic excellence cannot be the primary commitment of a seminary committed to professional education.

One of the primary functions of professional education is to nurture in the emerging professional an image of himself as a professional, an "occupational identity." The seminary, as a professional school, must be measured in terms of its effectiveness in doing this. Put most simply, the seminary must assist the student to move beyond his image of himself as a "student" and begin to see himself as a "minister." This does not mean he ceases to see himself as a learner. Rather, he learns how to learn when he is not in school. Put another way, the student must establish as his educational objective, not getting out of school, but getting into ministry. The educational efforts required to guide the student in this reformulation of his occupational identity will force significant changes in theological education. It raises serious questions about the adequacy of the "school model" for the theological seminary.

First, let me sketch my understanding of the process by which we have come to the academic model we have today. There was a time when (largely because of denominational rivalries and isolation) every individual seminary felt it had to have everything: history, theology, Hebrew, liturgy, Greek, philosophy—even astronomy, physics, and other elements of general education. Only a few universities had theological faculties, and most denominations would not trust the universities with their theology or their theological students. So every seminary, whether large or small, had to have a complete theological establishment or it felt unworthy and inadequate. The emergence of the American Association of Theological Schools has been a significant movement toward academic excellence. Its standards of accreditation encouraged the use of the academic model as the norm for all the seminaries.

But with the emergence of two significant developments in recent years, seminaries are set in a different context. First, the rise of graduate departments of religion in universities which make no pretense to interest either in Christian faith as a matter of orthodoxy or in Christian ministry as a matter of profession. Second, the emergence of training centers for ministry, offering a wide range of options for students and practicing professionals. In this new context the traditional seminary faces serious competition for students. At the same time it opens new educational opportunities for the seminaries. What is the function of a seminary when options for professional education exist outside the seminary? If a person wants to study religion and receive training for professional functions, he need not go to a seminary at all. He can go to a university for a graduate degree in religion, to an urban training center, to a program of clinical pastoral education, to management institutes and communications workshops, and be a very well-trained professional. In principle, at least, it is possible. It remains to be seen if the several churches will sanction this kind of professional education. But the impact on seminary admissions is likely to be significant—and soon. Admissions officers will have two important functions in relation to these developments. First, to interpret these changes to candidates for the profession. Second, to help the faculty and administration of the seminary to understand the import of these changes for the seminary, itself. One critical question concerns the continued use of the academic model for theological education.

My conviction is that the school model is not necessarily a bad model, if the clue we follow from higher education is the model of the graduate professional school, and not the model of the graduate academic department. The profession for which the seminary prepares is *ministry*, not religion or theology. And in a professional school the independent disciplines are drawn together by a common commitment to the profession. This professional commitment is a critical factor in the development of the occupational identity of the student.

The graduate professional school assumes responsibility to prepare intellectually and socially responsible leadership for a sector of society. Its primary commitment is not to prepare academic specialists who can reflect on questions and advise others, but to prepare professionals who will assume responsibility in society for the areas committed to their charge. A key concept is "leadership."

John Gardner wrote some years ago about the "leadership vacuum." He noted an increasing number of university graduates who wanted to be consultants and advisors, researchers and designers but not leaders and decision-makers. The academic model in higher education tends to reinforce this disposition to analysis, criticism, speculation, and detachment. Decision-making is very nearly the center of professional activity. Therefore a professional model for seminary education must include the assumption of responsibility and the making of decisions. This is what I mean when I say the seminary must help the student get over thinking of himself as a student and into the habit of thinking of himself as a professional.

But the seminary will have difficulty doing this. First of all, as I have noted before, there is pressure on the seminaries to use the academic model in securing faculty, designing curriculum, etc. But, second, the student has become an expert in playing his role in this system. It may be the only role he really knows. He has had to prove from nursery school onward that he can color within the lines, get his papers in on time, do what the teacher asks, and get good grades (at least C+ if he wants to go to seminary!). In the traditional academic department the three major skills required are: reading books, writing papers, and passing examinations. Some seminary faculty members think it is their function to help the seminarian get better at doing these three things—but at an advanced level. The problem is, of course, that as soon as the seminarian graduates he will never have to do these things again. Careful attention to the distinction between academic department and professional school will assist the seminary in designing an appropriate school model.

In addition to the academic system, the residential system is important. I personally feel that the monastic model will probably have to go. If it ever was a good model for Protestant theological education it certainly is questionable today. The old-style residential seminary prepared a minister to live in a dormitory with his peers, to eat his meals in a dining hall, and to worship in the seminary chapel. In the old days, we would not let students marry except in very special circumstances. So the residential system prolonged the undergraduate syndrome. Now we allow married students in the seminary, but either require or encourage them to live in the "seminary community," offering low-cost apartments handy to the classroom and chapel. But learning to live this way does not prepare students for life as professionals in society. Too many seminary graduates waste too much time during the early years of their ministries learning how to live outside the compound, with responsibility for establishing personal relations in the community at large. The seminary may have a need to fill its facilities, but the more important need of the student is to develop his occupational identity.

The "credit system" is another element in the kind of school model being employed. This involves more than "grades." It is related to the residential system in a very important way. In most schools the transfer student is penalized. If he changes schools he may lose credits, be required to complete additional work, and have to fulfill some kind of residence requirement in order to receive the degree of the institution. All this is designed to discourage movement of students from one school to another We could begin by inverting the reward-sanction system by rewarding the transfer student and, perhaps, penalizing the resident student. This kind of pressure may be necessary to "set" the student toward a style of professional education he can maintain in practice. Such a style is directly related to career development.

The emerging professional must learn how to continue his learning in relation to the resources that are around him. He will not spend the rest of his life in a school. He must learn how to learn when he is not in school. That is what I mean by "getting over being a student." As soon as he graduates he must be able to learn from his professional practice, in cooperation with other professionals in the community. This is why theological education should be carried on in relation to other professional schools, developing what I call "occupational ecumenicity." We have done pretty well with "ecclesiastical ecumenicity" in the seminaries, getting professors and students from different religious traditions together. Now we must make significant moves in the direction of inter-professional education, for this is the shape of professional practice in ministry. The seminary is the place where the student can begin to learn to do that.

Another point at which the school model and occupational identity come together is in "trial year" programs. The Rockefeller program is the best known among those which encourage students who are vocationally uncertain to come to seminary to see if they are interested in the ministry. I wonder if such a trial year ought to be in the seminary at all. Perhaps it should be an experience in the profession rather than in the professional school. The critical question is not whether he wants to be a theological student but whether, after being a theological student, he wants to be a minister. The seminary can assist in this search if it provides the student with more than professors for mentors. The student needs to be accountable to seniors in the profession. These are the professionals with whom students will be living and working. Students also need the assistance of laymen in their self-evaluation. Professors can be academic mentors, but the seminaries need a more inclusive system of advisors if the seminarian is going to get over thinking of himself as a student and begin responding to professional colleagues. I am hopeful that the Academy of Parish Clergy will work with the seminaries to develop some models for collegial relationships between seminarians and pastors. But the seminary faculties will have to learn how to relate to these non-academic colleagues if their students are to move toward a significant occupational identity as ministers.

To take occupational identity seriously means adopting a change model for the seminary. The school model on its academic side is really too rigid and resistant to change, too hung up on specialization, rank, and privilege. The research model will be useful if the research keeps the seminary close to changes in the church, community, and profession—and if theology can become theory for the profession and not simply another isolated academic discipline. But the model of the graduate professional school can be useful, since it is already an interdisciplinary faculty committed to research and teaching in the service of a responsible profession. Seminaries can take seriously the task of theological education as professional education by becoming accountable to the profession. They can assist the student toward an occupational identity as a minister and use career development as a model for theological education.

C. PASTORS AND PROFESSORS: PARTNERS IN MINISTRY

The key to these developments is a new kind of partnership between the seminary and the profession, between pastors and professors. We must involve pastors in the professional education of seminarians, not simply as adjunctive staff members supervising "field work," but as mentors to students in their search for professional identity and competence. This does not require that pastors become professors, or that professors become pastors. But it does require a partnership in which each party plays his role out of his own identity and integrity. Students in the seminary need to experience a variety of models and styles. The seminary community needs to become more inclusive and pluralistic. But this is not likely to happen so long as pastors continue in the conform/complaint syndrome, criticizing the seminary for its irrelevance but not providing any concrete alternatives. Nor will it happen while pastors continue in the bitch/brag syndrome, talking out of both sides of their mouths and plastering the seminary walls with pastoralia.

The future of the ministry and of theological education is in the hands of those who assume responsibility for it. I look for a new partnership between seminary and profession to shape that future.

Appendix: Sample Cases

Here are some additional sample cases from our files. They are not "ideal" or "typical." Cases vary with the pastors who prepare them. In every case we are dealing with a concrete pastoral event. These cases illustrate the variety of events that can be reported—even on one sheet of paper. Of course, more information becomes available as the "presenter" answers questions of the group. Sometimes we have rewritten the case after the discussion to include this additional information and to sharpen the description to make the dynamics of the event clearer. These cases are printed exactly as they were submitted to case conference groups.

SAMPLE CASE #3

BACKGROUND: The Young Adult Church School Class of my pastoral appointment is one of the most radically conservative groups I have ever seen. They almost have the John Birch outlook and approach. They strongly oppose the "socialistic trends" of the church, they have complained about the literature, and in general they gripe about every phase of the church and change. At the same time, the young adults are one of the most affluent groups in the church and community. This is due primarily to inheritance or becoming "partners" in an already established business belonging to parents. The former pastor stated to me that he did not work with this group as he should. He stated that he had neglected them. Previous to my coming to the appointment, I had been told that these people were unfriendly and arrogant. Therefore, when I arrived on the scene, this was one of areas in which I made my thrust. I began to meet regularly with them and attempted to cultivate their friendship.

DESCRIPTION: The Class asked me to do a series of sessions on the "Current Trends of the Church." I consented. During the first session, I laid the background that Christianity involves the whole man in all of society. I pointed out that this was the purpose of "Israel" and the message of the Bible, beginning with Amos. During all the sessions, I attempted to show that church history supports the movements of the church in contemporary society. After two sessions, the class began to question me regarding my personal beliefs concerning race, poverty, etc. I made an honest attempt to answer the questions with openness, understanding, and intelligence. Each time they would reply, "The church should apply itself to preaching the gospel." During the fourth session, one of the members with the support of the class began to compare me with the local Baptist minister and what he believes. When this continued through the fifth session, I called a halt, for I felt that the class was telling me what they wanted me to believe and how they wanted me to conduct myself in the parish and pulpit.

ANALYSIS: I am amazed that the people who have been given the most, often are the most critical of the "give away" programs. They object to the poor being on welfare for "the poor will not work." At the same time, I do not hear any criticisms about "give away" to the rich. This attitude has something to do with the attitude of the class, for not a member has come up through the ranks of hard work. I think that the class is more interested in their status than the gospel. They are more interested in making money than in giving, for the class has the lowest percentage of stewardship of any class in the church. They are using the "socialistic trends" as a method of escape from involvement.

EVALUATION: I don't know. Should I have consented to discuss such issues with the class, for I knew that it would be a risk? How can one win people whose minds are closed and whose hearts are hard concerning certain aspects of the church?

How can one be their friend and pastor without supporting them in their views? Very interesting.

SAMPLE CASE #4

BACKGROUND: In a previous pastorate of eight years' duration, there was a young couple with three children all of whom attended Sunday morning services fairly regularly. At one time during the eight years, the wife taught a Sunday school class. My association with the couple was fairly frequent in such events as athletics sponsored by the church and occasional social activities of a group nature. I was with them during the illness and death of the husband's father and preached the funeral. I visited in their home on a few occasions when there was special need and on a few other times to encourage them in more involvement in the church activities. As time passed and I was unable to win them to active participation in the total church program, I found myself growing resentful toward them, while there most certainly were a number of others I had not been able to win who were reacting in a similar fashion. Yet there was not the resentment present toward these others that I felt toward this particular couple. I suppressed the resentment and continued to try to show them friendliness when our paths crossed, but without any serious attempt to try to be a pastor to them.

DESCRIPTION: Now that I am in a different pastorate and just getting acquainted, I find similar feelings arising concerning a young couple I hardly know, whom I interpret to have similar feelings of disinterest in the church. I first recognized these feelings on Easter Sunday morning, when I noticed the couple smiling over some whispered humor during the most serious portion of the service. Already I feel alienated from them, yet I barely have gotten acquainted with them. I find myself not wanting to visit their home, not wanting to confront them even in a friendly fashion.

ANALYSIS: I am generally much more of an introvert than an extrovert and not usually aggressive. Because of this, one of my most threatening situations is in the area of personal confrontation with individuals who I feel need to be confronted with greater concern for the church and their personal Christian involvement. Perhaps I feel threatened because both seem to be making similar decisions, and perhaps I am angered because I feel this will reflect on me as a pastor.

EVALUATION: I know I will never win this couple as long as I feel as I do. Yet I am unable to resolve the conflict concerning my feelings toward them. How can I deal with this conflict effectively? Why is it I am more perturbed with some couples I am unable to win, than I am with some others? Why should I feel more threatened in some instances than in others?

SAMPLE CASE #5

BACKGROUND: This 385-member United Methodist Church is located in a small county seat town of 2,500 citizens. The church and community are very, very conservative in regard to the social change of our nation. This is Wallace Country. The local public school has been desegregated with 8 Negro teachers and 19 Negro students. This has caused a strong reaction to the federal system of justice, and a private school has been organized. All ministers except one (me) have expressed their support by attending the organizational meetings or by enrolling their children. I have indicated my support to the public school system. This support has been visibly expressed by my joining the quarterback club and by my wife doing substitute teaching. The community has also been informed that my children would attend the public school. In the very beginning of the organizational discussions for the private school, the pastor of another denomination volunteered to be the headmaster and offered his church for facilities of the school. The rumor came to me that the directors of the school would ask for some of our facilities.

DESCRIPTION: Immediately after hearing the rumor, I contacted the Church Lay Leader to give him all the reasons why the church—regardless of denomination—should not be involved in a private school program. I related to him all the problems which would be involved, the divisions that it would create within the membership, the destruction of property, the historical position of The Methodist Church in this Conference, and that it was our responsibility to serve *all* the people of the community—those in public schools as well as the ones who would attend the private school. This was a most frustrating and disturbing chore because he is on the Board of Directors and the chairman of the Finance Committee for the private school. However, he is devoted to his church and did not want the above problems to arise. (I hope.)

A week later, after the other church turned down their pastor and his position, by a vote of 55 to 54, and before the total community knew the decision of the other church, two of our more radical members of the Official Board came to me to persuade me to establish a private school. Again I told them all the reasons why the church should not be involved but with a stronger emphasis. The Church Lay Leader more recently mentioned to me that we may want to organize a school for the coming year on the basis that it will make money for the church. It seemed that a Methodist church in another town had influenced him at this point. Once more, I related to him that I was committed to Methodism and its current thrust, and that all Methodist schools must be racially inclusive. At this point the discussion was ended—and I hope forever.

ANALYSIS: The private school will divide the white community, and I fear will isolate the students. The majority of students will continue to attend the public school because of the expenses involved. The local KKK has offered their financial assistance, and only time will tell what will happen at this point. The other local church has already divided over the issue. What this does to the effectiveness of their pastor, I do not know and really do not care. I do not know what bearing this crisis will have on the local Methodist congregation; however, I do believe that it will handicap the financial support of our program.

EVALUATION: At the present time, I have come out of this ugly situation smelling like a rose, for I have not isolated the private school people. If I can convince the radical young adults that I care about them in spite of our disagreements, then I will have succeeded. At several points, I have even contributed advice to their program by reminding them of some of the problems that they will face. But only time will tell how they really feel. In 2 or 3 months, they could begin to criticise my visitation, my preaching, and the way I comb my hair. They will not attack the real issue. The financial support may decrease, and then the cabinet will look at the Conference reports rather than seeing that a Methodist Church has kept its conscience.

SAMPLE CASE #6

BACKGROUND: A large church located in what was formerly a desirable suburb which now is becoming a city neighborhood with all the implications this has. The one overpowering issue, however, is the advance of the Negro ghetto with the threat this poses for the community. An associate pastor has, since his recent arrival, been active in a group that has been trying to move Negro families into the community.

EVENT: An outside group chose our community and one realtor in particular to show how real estate interests were keeping the suburbs closed to Negro home-buyers. Local civil rights groups were asked to participate but not to plan the action and voted not to participate. The first event was a march of concerned clergymen from all over the metropolitan area. The associate pastor, at the last minute, decided to participate, and since he was one of the few local pastors so doing, he was featured in the march, in the newspapers, and over television. Scheduled to preach the following day, he delivered a sermon on an entirely different subject which people complained about strongly because they considered it an affront to their intelligence and to their commitment, a judgmental sermon with no compassion or understanding. As a result of both of these things, there was much hue and cry in the congregation with demands for the Associate Pastor's resignation and with some persons threatening to leave the church.

ANALYSIS: Although pastors had participated in other demonstrations before this, the congregation reacted so vehemently in this case because: (a) they believed the minister was being disloyal to the community. This was an outside group trying to bring shame to the community. (b) They considered him still an outsider himself since he had been there only a short time. (c) They had resented his previous activities and judgmental words against them. (d) His action touched upon the basic split that exists in the church today. The associate pastor acted in this way because: (a) He believed this would help the church and the community in facing the problem. (b) He had a sense of frustration over what he could "be" and "do" as a pastor. (c) He felt the pressure to conform to the image of the "active and involved pastor" that is placed before all of us today.

EVALUATION: As senior pastor, I attempted to minister to all involved: (1) The session: To help it face up to its responsibility to its ministers in aiding, counseling, and guiding them in their work, and in supporting them as persons. (2) The congregation: (a) To help it see the need for pastors to have freedom and to receive acceptance from the congregation. (b) To help it recognize this minister as an installed pastor with his own decisions to make and his own ministry to them. (c) To try to do these things directly and with the session. (3) The associate pastor: (a) To assure him of my support and of the session's in his decision. (b) To help him see some ways in which he could continue his ministry in the congregation with effectiveness. (c) To help him become secure enough so that he need no longer bring out his vocational frustrations in damaging ways. And finally, running through all this was the desire to use this event to help us all move forward in our facing up to how the church could act as the Church in this issue.

SAMPLE CASE #7

BACKGROUND: A recent meeting of the financial commission in an urban church of 450 members was called as a special meeting to discuss the financial crisis within the church. The church has been under a $100,000 bond issue for 10 years and still has 4 years to pay on the issue. They are paying $176 a week to building indebtedness. This church was organized in 1939. Its structure now consists of a small, inadequate sanctuary and a very fine educational building. The Sunday school has recently had over 200 in attendance for several Sundays, but the worship services have fallen off in attendance and the financial support has shown a decline over the past three years. This is the present minister's third year.

DESCRIPTION: The financial commission came to grips with part of the problem at its called meeting. It cut the present budget from $33,000 to $28,000. Most items were conference-related items. It has a record of very poor support of the conference. The commission is to have a special drive during December to inform the people of our present situation. The question was asked why had the "giving" become so deficient across the membership. The answer was, "Because of the trends in The Methodist Church, the liberal trends of race relations, National Council of Churches, etc."

ANALYSIS: It is interesting that these people expect the church to come to their rescue at the times of their personal crisis, but they are not willing to support it. Even the local bills have fallen behind. They were willing to have a "fish fry" to help pay for these bills, but little or no concern has been shown to pay any conference or missionary askings. The pastor borrowed $500 last year and $250 the year before to help pay for these askings.

EVALUATION: I now realize that these men's understanding of the work of the conference must be redefined. Their fears must be dispelled, and trust needs to be established between the laymen and the "conference." This will come through education and confrontation. It also will come through reevaluation of each member's commitment during the financial crisis. Many of the committee members expressed a real desire to ask people who are not supporting the church to leave. It is also the conclusion that paying their bills for them as a minister only protected my ego and did nothing for them as far as emphasizing their responsibility. I feel that the present crisis is good for the church and will be helpful in the long run.

SAMPLE CASE #8

BACKGROUND: Suburban church; 330 members; professional people, airline pilots, and salesmen; average age, 30; 1965 budget $30,000. The budget committee had proposed a budget for 1966 of $34,500. The canvass was conducted, but only $28,000 was raised from all sources. The budget committee chairman, a member of the session, decided along with the church treasurer to propose at the next session meeting a cutback of the proposed budget to $28,500. This decision was made without consulting the minister. When I learned what was coming, only minutes before the meeting, it was my hope to discourage any large cutback, as I felt the $34,500 was needed to continue the growth we had realized during 1965 in all phases of our church life and program.

DESCRIPTION: The budget committee chairman listed on the blackboard the original figures and his proposed cut for each committee. We discussed each committee in turn, with my arguing the cutback in every case. To a man, the session disagreed with me. It was as if they were saying, "We understand what you are saying pastor, but we disagree." The vote was finally taken, and the cutback was passed unanimously with one exception—a $500 figure for long-range planning which was to lead to the building of new church school facilities. I made it clear that when this budget was introduced to the congregation for their support my displeasure with the cutback would be announced.

ANALYSIS: As I've said, I did not anticipate this large cutback. The surprise threw me off guard, and I didn't recover until after the session meeting. The decision of the session reflected to me the spiritual stance of the congregation. We seem to be acting like a church of 100 members that is afraid to catch a vision and run with it for fear of overextending ourselves and losing what we have already accomplished. Yet we are in an extremely fast-growing suburb that nets between 500 and 1,000 people each month. The possibilities are great! As a congregation in this rapid growth situation, we have had a history of poor stewardship with resulting debt problems. I believe that the session in its decision was running out of fear of the past. They felt that past budgets were unrealistic, and this time they would propose nothing more than the people had demonstrated they were willing to pay. I found myself cast in the role of a prophet, discussing with them such concepts as "sacrificial giving," "faith," "not what we want, but what the Lord requires of us," etc. However, this did not influence their vote.

EVALUATION: Afterward, I asked myself, since I alone defended the original budget, was I wrong and were they right? I honestly believe I was right. Budget time is rolling around again. In preparing for this, I have noticed how weak our year-round stewardship interpretation is. What will I say from the pulpit? In and out of the pulpit I feel I must present the stewardship challenge in clear and unmistakable terms. Is part of the answer greater clarity on my part? I'm not sure. What does a pastor do when he finds himself standing against his people? Where does the element of faith enter with regard to a person's giving and the work of the church? How do you get across the necessity for spiritual growth in one's stewardship?